AN EMPTY SEAT IN CLASS

An Empty Seat in Class

teaching and learning
after the death of a student

Rick Ayers

TEACHERS
COLLEGE
PRESS

Teachers College
Columbia University
New York and London

Published by Teachers College Press, 1234 Amsterdam Avenue, New York, NY 10027

Library of Congress Cataloging-in-Publication Data available at www.loc.gov.

ISBN 978-0-8077-5612-6 (paper)
ISBN 978-0-8077-7348-2 (ebook)

Printed on acid-free paper
Manufactured in the United States of America

22 21 20 19 18 17 16 15   8 7 6 5 4 3 2 1

Contents

Acknowledgments

The writing of this book does not put me or anyone else in a celebratory mood. It's not a book anyone wants to have to write. Still, as time went on I became more and more committed to completing the project. So many people told me it was badly needed. I have so many people to thank for helping this project along the way. Some contributed long talks into the night, some shared stories, and some read various drafts. It has been such a long project that I'm sure I have left some of you out, but let me mention some dear comrades, colleagues, and just incredibly great people.

First, let me mention the teachers. I am in awe of each of you. No one who hasn't been there understands the struggle, dedication, and caring you bring every day: Noah Borrero, Godhuli Bose, Patrick Camangian, Amy Crawford, Father George Crespin, Julie Daniels, Biko Eisen-Martin, Trevor Gardner, Phil Halpern, Crystal Laura, Michelle Lee, Greg Michie, Hasmig Minassian, Leah Katz, Dana Moran, Bill Pratt, Dharini Rasiah, Fahim Johnson, Anjali Rodriguez, Tara Singh, Jaimie Stevenson, Dave Stovall, Marisa Morales, Susannah Bell, and Angelica Tolentino.

And let me add other readers and people I talked to about this; each of you is a treasure. First and foremost are my core family people, my editors and inspiration and number one cheerleaders: my brother Bill Ayers and my dear wife, Ilene Abrams. Also among the readers I count my brother John Ayers and my three wonderful children Aisha Ayers, Max Abrams, Sonia Abrams; and then the wonderful Jesse Alter, Sarah Biondello, Cori Bussolari, Bernardine Dohrn, Susan Katz, Grace Kim, Kevin Kumashiro, Avi Lessing, Susie Lundy, Cliff Mayotte, Grace Mungovan, Laura Popovics, Lisa Klope, Milton Reynolds, Joanne Ruby, Carole Saltz, Bill Sokol, Jean Ward, and Christine Yeh.

And I give special thanks, honor, and love to the families—they are the ones who carry the greatest burden. I can't name them all but must give a shout-out to Kimberly Willis-Starbuck, John Starbuck, Zachary Starbuck, Molly Starbuck, Felicia Jones, Cannon Jones, Cameron Jones, Craig Strang, Persis Karim, Niko Karim-Strang, Mercedes Ruiz, Tomio Denver-Nagano, Abby Mikael, and Dana Johnson.

A Teacher Holds on to a Dying Student

We were in Mexico when we heard. On vacation for a few weeks, quiet time at San Miguel de Allende. At 6:00 on Sunday morning, the fifth day of our stay, we got a phone call—who would be calling us here, and at this hour? Most of the time our cellphones didn't even work in Mexico. But it was our daughter Sonia who'd been housesitting for us, and her voice was urgent. She explained that she'd gotten phone calls, a bunch of them, in the middle of the night. "It was different students of yours calling the house. They said that someone named Meleia was shot . . ."

Suddenly I couldn't understand what she was talking about. Meleia? Did she mean a friend of hers? What Meleia? Who? Confused, I handed the phone to Ilene. As soon as she started speaking to Sonia, she let out a loud cry and crumpled to the ground, still cradling the phone to her ear. "Oh no, not Meleia, no." I was simply blocking out the news. Ilene got it right away. Meleia had been shot and killed on College Ave.

Meleia was an African American student who had graduated from our social justice–oriented small school—Communication Arts and Sciences (CAS) at Berkeley High School—2 years earlier. She was living in Berkeley and doing an internship at the Women's Daytime Drop-in Center. We had seen her only a week before at Mercedes' baby shower—a little early to have a baby, we worried, but clearly this one was surrounded by a world of support, the first among them being the godmother-to-be Meleia. As we left the shower, Ilene had arranged a lunch date with Meleia for soon after we were scheduled to get back.

1

The details don't really matter. Well, they matter supremely, but there is no need for them now. Just that it had been 2 A.M.; Meleia got shot through the heart by a .38 mm bullet from a handgun. Gang violence? A robbery gone wrong? We did not know. She died right where she fell on College Avenue.

We wandered around the San Miguel locales that had been so serene and sweet just moments before: the café, and the yellow and ochre plaza in front of the church. Now everything had a pall over it; everything signaled death. We found a photo of Meleia online and printed it out, fashioning a little altar with a votive candle. We called and talked to Mercedes, to Rafael, to fellow teachers. Too much was happening. Too much was needed. We arranged a flight out of León for the next night.

As soon as we got to Oakland, we drove to the tree next to which Meleia had been shot. It was already a makeshift memorial—we gazed at the extended pile of candles, flowers, mementos. We read the tributes, viewed the photos, beginning the day of tears—it was a relief to finally be there.

We went to the funeral home where there was a viewing all day. Meleia's parents were living in Georgia and would not arrive for another day. It was all the kids and the teachers for now. Goapele's song "Closer" was playing over and over. I only remember a montage of faces, coming into focus from the background; encounters, looks of disbelief, melting between former identities. The first kid I hugged was Rafael, appropriately; he'd been a key force through all this, talking to me on the phone in Mexico; he had been just the right combination of totally present in his grief and completely tuned into and looking out for others. Next hug: Hiroshi, always by Rafa's side, big and bear-like. Both hugs were long and slow, and silent. Ilene was holding others, barely visible in the trembling mass. Then it was Pera—she just broke down, cried and cried, deep shaking sobs into my chest. Some moment came for each person at the funeral home that afternoon when they finally let go. This pushed me over, too. Pera finally gave way and turned to hug Eden—who was around all day with her sister Abby. Their wonderful Eritrean mother was there later, too. Nico and his mom. And it went on.

Bill Pratt showed up, and I was so glad to see my colleague and fellow teacher, the anchor in all this for the whole week. Our Sonia had phoned him right after us on Sunday morning. She had had to tell Beth, as Pratt was out on a ride. Beth was knocked over; she knew Meleia from the Vietnam trip we all took together. We had a big hug. Nhu arrived. Others.

Then we left for a meeting with some adults and students, those who loosely were forming the steering committee to plan the memorial for Friday. We also had to deal with media, as the narrative they were telling was drifting into the "all bad Black youth" version, their vans hanging around vulture-like. The meeting was chaotic as it was constantly interrupted by phone calls, crises, and logistical side roads. The kids had worked out a speaker list the night before and then there were family members, college friends who had flown out, and politicians.

We agreed that the politicians who wanted to speak would mostly be cut. We had to focus on the young people and the family, and on Meleia. It was not going to be an opportunity for face time for politicians who never knew Meleia to try to look like caring leaders. It was a time to confront the mystery and horror and sorrow of death (no easy, comforting clichés) and it had to also be a celebration of a life.

We returned to the funeral home for a gathering of family and close friends, for some words to be spoken. Lots more kids, parents, long and urgent embraces. Anye and her mom, Valerie; Arose and Danielle; Hannah; Sean and his dad, Henry. When Henry wrapped me in those big powerful arms for a long bear hug, I finally exhaled and sobbed unrestrained, feeling somehow safe and supported (held up) rather than being the supporter.

And Tomio, another incredible anchor, incredible friend. After Meleia was killed, the kids who were together realized that someone had to tell her mom, Kimberly, who was living in Atlanta. Or they would have to let the cops do it. It was a long, hard decision. It came down to Tomio or Mercedes. One of the students asked him to please do it. After some thought, he said, "Okay." It was the worst assignment, a horror. But he called her, and Kimberly still thanks him for being the one to do it.

When we went back to the tree later, we saw Sophie, the other Hannah. More touching and holding. Katie and her sister, hugs again. Katie has been a real keeper of the memorial and was busy lighting and moving candles. Finally, we went home. Later we stopped by the memorial again. Saw Eden, Leah, Abby, Dana, and a bunch of others. And there was an after-gathering at Gabby's folks' house. Mostly, we all just wanted to be together.

Introduction

To just sit down and begin to write, to try to begin to write, about the death of a student is appalling. Appalling that the deaths of young people have become a commonplace, an everyday occurrence about which we need to have a dialogue. But also appalling because losing a student is a howling nightmare, an unmitigated horror, leaving little more than a gaping emptiness and mystery, something beyond words. But words are what we have. Writing, summarizing insights, was the furthest thing from my mind in those first weeks; as the months and years went by, I turned to words as a solace and a way to acknowledge this dreaded experience as part of what teachers do.

Here's the amazing thing: Nearly every teacher I talk to about student death is eager to tell his or her story, is still reliving the experience and all its complicated channels and side stories. My dear wise friend Dana Moran recently wrote me:

> I don't know what to say because I have never "learned" anything from any loss of a student, and have absolutely no words of wisdom for a young teacher experiencing it for the first time. I have only love and sympathy in a world gone crazy. We fight for these kids and their lives one kid at a time and, try though we might, we cannot protect them any better than we can protect our own children. Our vulnerability is multiplied a hundred times every year that we teach. I've been at it for 27 years and still have anxiety

attacks and bad dreams about kids who have dangerous lives, and I still cry when I talk about Canon or Meleia or Keith. . . . I have started calling this an "occupational hazard" and it is the price we sometimes pay for loving the kids we work with. But to not love them is worse—and to not fight for/with them is unthinkable.

And that is just about all you can say. Reading Dana's words and sharing her feelings has made me stop this project quite a few times. I thought at the time that there are no words. Good teaching recognizes that each child is a unique being in the universe—no one else has ever been or ever will be the same as this person. The very singularity, the irreplaceable ending that is this death, makes it seem blasphemous to draw any general conclusions. Abstraction itself belittles the tragedy.

But as an English teacher, as someone who believes that our salvation lies more in literature and stories than in psychology and political analysis, in time the words kept coming. Lots and lots of words—talking, wondering, reading, talking again. It was both a mourning and a shaping, an attempt to harness reality to a story, any story, that would make sense.

> The very singularity, the irreplaceable ending that is this death, makes it seem blasphemous to draw any general conclusions. Abstraction itself belittles the tragedy.

So I will tell you what this book is not: It is not a "how-to" book because there are no clear answers. Rather, it offers the experiences of teachers to help colleagues and communities find their own way. It is not a policy prescription about gun violence or the much-needed analysis of oppression and inequity in our society. These underlying issues are inescapable when one looks at the news reports, but they are not the primary concern of this book. In this book I pay a lot of attention to the epidemic of deaths by gun violence in U.S. cities. But, as I have talked to colleagues, I have realized that we go through similar crises and work when a student dies in a car accident; we share the sorrows in the long process of a student dying from illness; and we are particularly thrown off by the sad surrender of suicide. So I have devoted some space to all of these issues. Writing about this journey is not an artful or graceful or redeeming recasting of the experience. But let the words take us where they will, help us illuminate our way in the valley of the shadow of death.

This is a meditation with and for teachers, on the teaching profession and how we do our jobs in these terrible moments. Counselors are often much better at this and understand it more deeply. But schools are set up in such a way that counselors are isolated from the classroom and mostly do one-on-one work with students, while teachers are quarantined away from social and emotional support. So let us take a moment for teachers to talk, think, and struggle with what to do when students die. It is a reflection for parents and kids as well. The death of a student is a raw wound, a pain that never goes away, never finds that elusive and clichéd "closure," but only becomes, thankfully, something further in the past. Until the next time.

This moment makes us think deeply about the position of teachers in these students' lives and in communities. For one thing, we are not family yet we have a family-like intimacy with our students. Like parents, we approach students with feelings of unconditional love. Unconditional love means being on their side no matter what, even when they make mistakes or do terrible things. They are our students and we are fighting for them and for the possibility that they will make the right choices. Not that we even know, every time, what the right choices are in their lives and their circumstances. We do not have a prescriptive sense of what they should do, but we are passionate about helping them pursue their own analysis, develop their own strategies for their lives.

Teachers have told me that when a student dies they are seized with the desire to get out of the profession, to quit, to get away. I remember thinking during the mourning for Meleia that if I had remained a restaurant cook, if I had not gone into teaching, I would have simply read about this death and shook my head. How sad, I would have thought, and that would have been it. But this. This pain. It was too much. Would I be subjected to it again and again? *I'm not sure I can do this.* That was the first feeling I had, and it lasted some time. But in time it dawned on me that we only feel this searing pain if we love someone. The cost of loving deeply is opening oneself up to that pain. And love is worth the pain—it affirms that we are alive. We were all in this messy, awful, roiling stew of pain, and it was a space suffused with love.

For teachers, who are going to love thousands of students in their lifetimes, the pain and loss is not just likely—it is inevitable. That may seem a little distancing, like getting some "professional perspective." But I don't mean it that way at all. It is as deep and painful and horrible as ever. But it is the world of teaching; it is the life we have signed up for. If you deeply care for, if you love your students, they will always break your heart, too. Your hopes are so high, if not for traditional straight As then at least for commitment or engagement. And students will disappoint, will insult, will lash out—just as angry teenage children do. They hurt you. But you continue to hope. When a student dies, it is the ultimate heartbreak. But, again, as with your own kids, you learn that teaching is not just adding in; it is also letting go, giving away. Our communities connect and then fragment. And we make the best we can of it.

Teachers, even deeply student-centered teachers, are so often the Prosperos of the classroom, the ones who construct the stage, set out the script, and set the action in motion. We define things and name things. With the death of a student, our utter powerlessness is exposed. Then I think of the words of Viktor Frankl (1984) in *Man's Search for Meaning*: "When we are no longer able to change a situation, we are challenged to change ourselves" (p. 135). This tragedy asks us to, forces us to, change ourselves.

Teachers are not first responders, lawyers, politicians, psychologists, or cheerleaders. But we have to be a little of all these things in the real world of classrooms and schools. It may seem wise to "send them to the counselor" or "get a shrink" when certain challenges come up. But the truth is that we must wear these various hats every day. The professionalization of skills (social worker, therapist, discipline dean, and so forth) seems reasonable but it ends up forcing us into silos. On some level, effective teaching must involve a bit of all of these practices—as we are whole adults dealing with whole young people. But in teacher education, in professional development, in all our work, we do not really have an extended conversation about what happens, what to do, when a student dies.

So, although this book is not a "how-to" for pre- or inservice teaching, Chapter 9 is in fact titled Teacher Education. In this book I hope to encounter my teaching colleagues where we are, in the messy complexity of our teaching lives.

The life of a teacher is always a balancing act. Teaching the subject matter, creating community, and being a little bit of a therapist, counselor, and mama at the same time. Instead of viewing this as a fragmented, unfocused reality, we can begin to understand the unique and important place that the teacher, holding space with her class, plays in this contingent collage of the human dance.

It always seems disembodied and irresponsible when the principal comes on the PA system and drones, "Grief counselors will be available in the gymnasium for those who need them." This gesture suggests that grief is so individual, the treatment of it so professionalized and specialized, that there is nothing for the community, the classroom, to do together. I also feel great sympathy for the counselors, for the specialists, who are kept out of the classroom and the general student community, isolated in offices doing scheduling, and then called upon at moments of crisis to work their magic. Our learning communities should not be so segmented.

> The life of a teacher is always a balancing act. Teaching the subject matter, creating community, and being a little bit of a therapist, counselor, and mama at the same time.

In the Afterword, I invite a first-rate counselor and therapist, one who has worked with grief and loss in schools, to address our need to be able to discuss death.

It has been many years since Meleia died and there have been other devastating losses since then—Canon Jones shot during a petty street stick-up; Kyle and Prentiss in a car accident. But I think perhaps I have enough distance from that first, defining tragedy to try to say something useful. As I was just beginning to write this book, 15-year-old Jubrille Jordan— a student I got to know as I observed and supported her student teacher—was shot and killed on a Sunday afternoon; on April 9, 2013, 19-year-old Dimarea Young, an artist and poet involved with Richmond's RAW Talent program, was shot and killed while taking a break at a job-training program; and then on May 5 Berkeley High and Castlemont High student Olajuwon Clayborn was gunned down in East Oakland. The bodies are piling up.

Everyone experiences death, sometimes searing painful deaths of family members, friends, or people we care about. We turn to psychology, religion, literature, philosophy, even politics to make some sense of it. The death of a student is the same and different in crucial ways. It is time we talk about this openly, explore it thoughtfully.

An Empty Seat in Class examines what teachers, what school communities can do or what we aspire to do or what we wish we could do when students die. I invite you into the consideration of many aspects of this terrible experience in the hopes that our shared conversation can make our teaching lives more effective and bearable. Finally, in Chapter 10, I have summarized many of the thoughts, suggestions, and ideas that have emerged in the creation of this book. Note that I have sometimes used real names when it was a matter of public record or when I obtained releases, but I have used fictionalized names in some cases in the interest of privacy.

1. Improvising

The memorial for Meleia was held at the school gymnasium on Friday. There were close to 1,000 people there. Chinaka, Bill, and I were MCs. We had mostly young people speaking, and some singing and music (Goapele herself came and sang; Sean Erick played "God Bless the Child" on his trumpet); and family; and a few teachers. Meleia's beautiful parents were there, barely able to look up. Her siblings Zack and Molly, bewildered. The students made a sign, replacing the traditional "rest in peace" with "REST IN POWER." A way to invoke Meleia's militant and deep spirit.

Over the period of a few weeks, the students found myriad ways to support one another, created memorials and memories, stood up together. They sang songs, danced, hiked, and wrote pieces to share out loud.

Rafael offered a poem:

Thank you for drivin' that fly-ass classic car that you bought
For the lessons you don't even know that you taught
For hotel party endeavors
For kickball games with cliques that never used to be able to kick it together
Smoke breaks on the scaffold outside your spot
Thank you for being such a rock
Thank you for bringing me round something like Daniel's smile
Or Anthony Washington's inhuman sense of style
For the brother I've found in Tomio

For all the folks I've grown to know
For the culture you bred and community you kept
For the love around the tree that everybody left
Thank you for being such a mother
For giving hugs that were slightly longer than others
See you were a hero and most didn't ever know it
Cuz see a true hero makes you feel like you're the one who is heroic

And Chinaka, trying to start her semester at college, wrote:

there isn't anyone i want to cry on here. i don't feel like explaining. so i find myself waiting until breaks in RA training, sobbing in bathroom stalls, or unabashedly down crowded streets. anything to keep from showing signs of weakness in front of these people who want to counsel, i just want to be silent, or talk to the hims who can't hear me. yo. I can't shake all these getaway cars in the bay. every thought is coupled with an anger about the disposable quality of young black life.

Students sat in circles. Took turns sharing memories or artifacts. Pera hung a butterfly ornament on the tree outside her house, recalling the ways that a chrysalis and butterfly had been metaphors for these young people as they were going through their teenage years. I realized they were reenacting some of the practices from our retreats and community building. They were finding a way, showing the way, invoking the memory of our time together to take the next steps, now, in crisis. We were, it seems, turning to our own community-building activities, our own classroom traditions, to improvise our way to a memorial that would be meaningful and helpful.

I was proud of them—and humbled. What these students had to build their mourning practice on was simply the community we had constructed when we were all together in that high school class, in our small school within a school. Again like family, we did not just study together; we did not just administer and take tests. There was the intimacy of knowing one another well. This meant finding the good and valuable in each person; it meant recognizing the flaws—the short temper, the cheating or exploiting, the depression—and caring for one another still.

We adults did our best but in the end our best did not consist of any particular advice, any directions given. It was mainly a matter of being present, being with them, and giving them space and agency to construct the next steps—it was exactly like the best of teaching; it was what the students had wanted out of their education all along.

Our public schools are secular institutions, one of the last gestures in our society of a commitment to a public good or even a public space. They are sites of contention and often creativity, places where we work out what we mean by democracy, what kind of world we want to live in, what kind of world we want our children to live in. We are a society of diverse and even conflicting cultural traditions and practices. School does not operate in a homogenous world where all students belong to the same religious institution with their comforting and tried traditions to process a death—sitting Shiva, praying the rosary, performing the Janazah, practicing Amitabha. When a student dies, certainly families and communities invoke their own cultural responses, and these may be observed quietly or on a canvas writ large. But the school community also must respond, must enter the heartbreak of it and find a way to repair the gash in the social fabric. Teachers generally must improvise and invent their own rituals, their own practices that include everyone in the room.

> We are a society of diverse and even conflicting cultural traditions and practices. School does not operate in a homogenous world where all students belong to the same religious institution with their comforting and tried traditions to process a death.

Good teaching is a series of questions—questions asked of the students and questions the teacher asks herself. When teaching is reduced to a series of declarative sentences, it becomes dull and flat. The habit of open-ended questioning is something that teachers cultivate over time, and there is never a time when that practice must be invoked more than when a crisis like this strikes.

When a classroom community is hit with the death of a student, the first thing many students want to do is get together. Sometimes they end up at someone's house, even a teacher's house, and sit up all night. As students figure out what they want to do together, they rely on and reproduce the practices and traditions that have characterized their class. If previously the group engaged in artwork, the art supplies will come out. If it is a class that did circle time, students will form a circle. Familiar practices seem to find their way into the space. This also means that a classroom that has been emotionally arid, that has been cool and distant, will not likely be a place where students can find help in processing the loss.

This reminds us that our work in building classroom communities, our regular routines and the culture of the group, is the crucial everyday responsibility of the teacher. We don't do the community building to get ready for a death. Community is central to our identity as humans as well as a critical ingredient for deep learning. But the community is also in place in times of crisis. Pera crying on my shoulder; me crying on Henry's shoulder—those moments were only possible because of the years of work that went before.

When we build classroom community in the Communication Arts and Sciences small school, for instance, we take a number of intentional steps beyond just the first day icebreaker activities. Students write and talk and explore about their own identity, about issues of their lives, and about their feelings about school. From initial guarded postures at the beginning of 9th grade to deep engagement across borders in 11th grade, students find their way to trust. Certain practices that were thought up as simple "camp-type" activities—such as the "artifact sharing circle"—become traditions that each class expects to experience on their 2-day retreat to the Marin Headlands. Only a few years before she was killed, Meleia shared a photograph and the story of her younger brother—exploring his struggles with learning differences and his resilience and loving presence in her life. We teachers can still remember the stories

of the artifact sharing from every class—from the tough football player who cried when describing his father's death to the
quiet student who brought the old suitcase his grandfather had
carried into the Japanese American relocation camp in 1942
and fiercely evoked that struggle. Artifact sharing, buddy walk,
journal time, apologies and appreciations—all these were part
of the creation of a school community that inspired unity and
commitment from these students. This is the community we
need when we are in crisis.

In social justice education, we help students think about
social ethics, about the choices we make and their consequences. We explore the terminology of *victim, perpetrator,*
and *bystander.*[1] When an injustice is done, large or small, generally people fall into one of those categories, though we also
slip and slide between these stances in different situations. But
we also imagine a time when someone is something else—we
used to say "rescuer" but that sounded too melodramatic. So
we call this person an upstander, someone who actually takes
a stance for justice, who intervenes or acts for the greater good.
Often, the examples of upstanders are heroic—someone stop-
ping a fight, intervening against an attack. We have to caution
against a Superman model of taking a stand for justice. More
than the moment of crisis, more than the heroic gesture, being an upstander is enacted in the day-to-day, in the values
and orientations and actions you take before the crisis. To be
an upstander in school might mean something as big as large
projects of community organizing or as small as speaking out
against a bully or refusing to allow someone to be designated
as "other" and ostracized.

Learning how to act as upstanders, learning to be in solidarity with students and the community, is the most important
practice a teacher will build on while groping for something to
do in response to the death of a student. An upstander attends
to the needs of the community as the most important way to

1. For excellent materials on this approach to curriculum, see Facing History and
Ourselves, www.facinghistory.org

enact her values. Students, teachers, parents—everyone learns this practice very quickly when tragedy strikes.

Even while teachers are in utter shock, are forced to look into the great empty abyss of death, are reaching out to the student who is gone, they are quickly reminded of their responsibility to the rest of the students, those who desperately need something to hold on to.

My own instinct here is to not offer a political analysis of the reason for the death, to not give prescriptions or speeches or answers right then. That can come later and it must be done. The way communities are oppressed, the operation of an economic system that ejects them, the racism of the school and court systems, the suicidal core of gun violence—all these need to be addressed. But not now, not right away. Students need the right to sit with the enormity of the loss, to focus on sending off their friend with full honors and attention. And most fundamentally, they must be acknowledged, they must be in a place of trust and honesty.

2. The Mystery

At Meleia's memorial, most speakers reminded us of this wonderful, vibrant, irreplaceable member of our community. And that was just right. But I felt suddenly the need to address the others, the kids who were being washed away in a flood of grief, who were unmoored and frightened by the mystery and the horror of death, to give them a branch to hang on to. So this is all I said:

> Many feel the terrible weight of this loss,
> Many of us have asked, why not me, I would rather die than see Meleia die
> Many have thought, death is so simple, such a short step over the edge,
> That they even have felt like dying.
> But you won't.

I can tell you that you won't get over it; the pain does not really go away. It just becomes something that you live with, something that is further and further in the past. But it is the same pain.

You won't die, you will live a long life, and you will grow old, and pass on in your good time.

And when you are old, and gray, and sitting by the fire, you will think back.

You will remember this wonderful young woman, Meleia Willis-Starbuck,

Who died way too early at 19.

And you will reflect that you lived a better life, a more compassionate life, a more meaningful life, because of her. And you will thank her for her example and for what she compelled you to do with your one precious life. And you will realize that all these well-lived lives, from all these hundreds of people assembled in this room, will be the legacy, will be the way that Meleia's great promise was fulfilled and carried out—it will have been through your lives. And for that we thank you ahead of time.

This is not your everyday Monday when a death in the class has occurred. And you need time, you must take time, to give it focus. To be in the presence of death is to confront the ultimate mystery. Various spiritual and philosophical traditions regard it differently but everybody is in awe, in fear, and in reverent attentiveness in the face of death. In teacher training, sex and death are pretty much taboo conversations—though they are said to occupy about 80% of our conscious and subconscious thinking.

While I was writing this book, my brother Tim died after an incredibly brief struggle with cancer. Once again the horror, once again the powerlessness. He was not a student, no, but he was family, which is another kind of tragedy. His friends showed up at the hospital; family rushed in. We managed to get him home with hospice care, a hospital bed and an oxygen machine in his dining room. As we sat up with him all night, taking turns holding his hand, gazing at him, speaking softly to one another, I felt the same awe as I had felt being at a birth. We were there to witness, to launch him out of this mortal plane. Like a birth, it was a matter of waiting and watching; it was a life transition; it was a transformation that was beyond our understanding; it was humbling and scary and . . . beautiful. At these moments we gaze into the portal, the doors between this existence and something quite other. It was frightening and yet I would much rather be there than just imagine it. Sitting right there certainly did nothing to lessen the mystery of it.

Some people are comforted by organized religion, with a clearly prescribed explanation of every step that happens after death. Some people prefer to sit with the uncertainty. Sometimes we shudder in fear, worrying about the great void of death spread before us; other times we talk about it cavalierly. But it is one thing for certain: a mystery. Only because we are conscious, meaning-making animals can we think about our impending deaths. This is the moment of imperative existential verdicts. And it is always unsettling.

> Sometimes we shudder in fear, worrying about the great void of death spread before us; other times we talk about it cavalierly. But it is one thing for certain: a mystery.

When my first child, Aisha, was born, I was struck with an exploding epiphany. This, this having of children, this miracle of birth. People everywhere do this, have done this. And for all of our competition for success in the world, for all we are proud to achieve in jobs or activism or scholarship, this, this basic thing, is the greatest accomplishment we could make. And everybody, or just about everybody, can do it. A few years later, with the kids in their raucous and delightful early childhood, I spent some months having nightmares about my own death, the abyss of it, the eternal nothingness of it. Once I managed to tame these nightmares something worse struck me: This abyss, this death, will come to my laughing and loving and dancing children some day. Even if it is when they are old, they will have to do it. Death is the serial killer that no one escapes. Our only small consolation is that it should come late. The death of a child is unspeakable.

Aleksandar Hemon (2011) wrote, when faced with the death of his own daughter:

There's a psychological mechanism, I've come to believe, that prevents most of us from imagining the moment of our own death. For if it were possible to imagine fully that instant of passing from consciousness to nonexistence, with all the attendant fear and humiliation of absolute helplessness, it would be very hard to live. It would be unbearably obvious that death is inscribed in everything that constitutes life, that any moment of your existence may be only a breath away from being the last. We would be continuously devastated by the magnitude of that inescapable fact. Still, as we mature into our mortality, we begin to gingerly dip our horror-tingling toes into the void, hoping that our mind will somehow ease itself into dying, that God or some other soothing opiate will remain available as we venture into the darkness of non-being.

But how can you possibly ease yourself into the death of your child? For one thing, it is supposed to happen well after your own dissolution into nothingness. Your children are supposed to outlive you by several decades, during the course of which they live their lives, happily devoid of the burden of your presence, and eventually complete the same mortal trajectory as their parents: oblivion, denial, fear, the end. They're supposed to handle their own mortality, and no help in that regard (other than forcing them to confront death by dying) can come from you—death ain't a science project. And, even if you could imagine your child's death, why would you?

A year after Meleia died we held a gathering for everyone who had been there that night, and for a number of others who had been close to her. Just before the gathering, I was driving around with my student Chinaka, finishing up details. We were listening to her mix tape of the blues. "I'd rather go blind," "Walking blues." I thought that at the heart of the blues is not really melancholy but rather a kind of uplift, even joy. What an odd thought. Was there joy? Certainly I could feel the performance of the blues as a collective sharing of pain, a reminder that suffering is not ours alone. The African American tradition of the blues was not invented to turn away from trouble; it was a way to sing us through trouble.

On this journey of life we must confront what it means to live in the world. So much of literature and art is created to convey this, but it takes a long time to understand it. Is there a way to make our lives properly in tune with the joy and pain of the world?

Native American author Louise Erdrich (2006) flings this truth in our face. She writes,

> Life will break you. Nobody can protect you from that, and living alone won't either, for solitude will also break you with its yearning. You have to love. You have to feel. It is the reason you are here on earth. You are here to risk your heart. You are here to be swallowed up. And when it happens that you are broken, or betrayed, or left, or hurt, or death brushes near, let yourself sit by an apple tree and listen to the apples falling all around you in heaps, wasting their sweetness. Tell yourself you tasted as many as you could. (p. 274)

Ah. The sweetness that was wasted, the lives not lived, the children not conceived and born. How could this happen? The only thing left is to taste and celebrate the sweet apples, and to plant more. In some ways, all literature, all art, all seeking the answer, is preparing for death. Some sketch out scenes that propose answers to the great unknown. But one of the tasks of art is really just to allow us to look over the great abyss. It is not to give certainty but to abide in the mystery.

But we must do things, we must put one foot in front of the other, even as we have these thoughts of wonder. And we do. Some schools put out butcher paper for students to write dedications on; others build altars—beautiful collections of art and candles and photographs and artifacts of a life. The phenomenon of the "RIP T-shirt" is now a cultural commonplace in the cities, with shops that cater to youth death as the main part of their business. As Principal G. Reyes of Arise High School in Oakland said to me, "Sadly, we know all too well how to do this."

And how we do this is to tell stories—to ourselves and to others. We make sense of the world through stories, through ongoing narratives of what we are doing, where we fit. But we view a narrative, and we tell a story, in different ways as we grow. I remember reading James Agee's tremendous novel *A Death in the Family* (1957) while in high school. It is the story of the deep and painful impacts the death of a father has on a small Midwestern family. My first reaction, however, was, "What a neurotic family; how horrible they are; no one can even talk to each other." I was, you see, a teenager with a highly attuned nose for criticizing hypocrisy and awkwardness in the family. I was working out my own anger with my family. I reread Agee's book 25 years later and saw a whole different story. "How excruciating," I thought. "How painful and dislocating is the experience this poor family is going through." Now I was not so worried about repressed emotions, having weathered my own creation of my own imperfect but very real family. Now I noticed the unspoken pain, the badly articulated suffering they were going through.

And I could feel, even in the repressed emotions, even in the unspoken thoughts, the way people need one another. We often talk in education about the need to build community. But this is more than a teaching strategy. Community, our caring in the presence of others, is what makes us human, what allows for love and sacrifice and meaning in the face of evil. Although the policy wonks posit us each as individual agents competing against others for the goodies, in the world that matters, it is love that matters.

We each tell our story in different ways through time. It is an evolving narrative. A childhood memory that seemed terribly traumatic at one point may become instructive or even humorous years later. We never get over the death of a loved one, a family member. But the narrative changes—sometimes in ways that are more bearable, while other times they become more painful.

Again, the students so often understand themselves clearly in this process; they find a way. Here is what high school student Grace Mungovan said at graduation, a little over a year after CAS junior Kyle Strang died in an auto accident, and their teacher Hasmig Minassian went through the unthinkable journey with the kids:

> Just as death cut through us and intensified our interactions with our lives, a second force, both older and more powerful than death, rose to complete the process. A force that turns profound life riddles into poems and illuminates meaning in chaos was activated deep within us to transform the broken pieces of the collective heart. The type of love that emerged in the community was love that had already been present; built within the infrastructure of the program and laying latent as potential within the nervousness of our freshmen smiles. Our heartbreak created a shift in the air, in our perspectives, in our psyches. This shift revealed what had been waiting for us as we grew. When the normalcy of our days was destroyed and time itself seemed to distort, a new kind of self emerged from each and every one of us; a self only present before in the glimmers of electricity that tease every soul.

These are young people growing up. From the timid and tentative entry into high school in 9th grade to their time of graduation, they have learned something as ancient as life and as current as today. In the face of the mystery, we lean on one another in awe.

The Literacy of Loss: Youth Creation of RIP T-shirts

Lanette Jimerson

Lanette Jimerson is director of the Multicultural Urban Secondary English (MUSE) credential and master's program at the University of California, Berkeley.

Gun violence in urban neighborhoods has resulted in what some have termed a murder economy. Newspapers, T-shirt shops, websites, songs, balloon companies, florists, mortuaries, and churches have profited from the death of victims of gun violence.

Overwhelmingly the victims of gun violence are Black and Brown young adult males.

The local practices of youth and adults creating Rest in Peace (RIP) T-shirts began in the 1990s at the height of the drug epidemic. In major urban cities such as Miami, Chicago, Detroit, and Oakland, where 131 people died in 2012, 118 of them from gun violence (56 of whom were ages 15–25), RIP T-shirts sustain a number of small businesses. In Oakland more than 30 T-shirt shops exist, mostly mom-and-pop-type storefronts, sometimes as a side business for another entity, such as the T-shirt shop inside of Doug's Tattoos; the locations of these T-shirt shops are generally only known to neighborhood residents. Oakland resident Aswad Hayes is said to be one of the first businessmen nationally to make RIP T-shirts, now an everyday clothing item in urban communities. He credits the RIP T-shirt to a hip-hop film, *I'm Bout It* (1997), about the life of Master P and his brother Kevin Miller. In the film Master P dons a RIP T-shirt with color photos of his brother who was killed during a robbery in 1990.

From 1999 until the present, RIP T-shirts have become a central grieving artifact for youth in low-income neighborhoods; a mobile altar of grief and loss.

The RIP T-shirts highlight the value and achievements of the deceased through photos and quotes: graduation from high school, loving relationships, hobbies, and pursuits. Often the shirts re-create the life of victims of violence from one of lack and despair to abundance, value, and joy. Created through iron transfers and digital scanners, the T-shirts often act as unofficial obituaries and validate the relationship of the owner of the shirt to the deceased. Often alienated during funerals in which pastors and adults berate young people for the violence in the community, youth have few spaces to narrate the pain of loss. Classrooms also provide few opportunities for youth to process the experience of loss, as the violent death of youth is a taboo topic in schools. These T-shirts represent out-of-school literacy practices in which students engage to cope with the loss of a peer; such literary practices are generally excluded from the education that we ask students to make a priority. Youth wear the T-shirts to make visible their pain and grief.

Often students of color are believed to lack the critical skill of analyzing characters and motivation, yet the practice of creating RIP T-shirts directly contradicts this supposition. Not only do youth defend their RIP T-shirt designs, but they often create co-constructed texts from either discussion with peers or the adaptation of spiritual and secular texts such as quotes from the Bible or sayings placed on posters and cards.

The RIP T-shirt allows students to critically reflect on the loss of a loved one, the structures of inequality, the destruction of violence, the resulting emotional trauma, and the ways in which humans reframe a person's life to cope. They encourage an understanding that even painful experiences can develop not only their ability to respond to trauma but also their ability to critically analyze the world in the terms of mainstream America—a must for urban students.

3. Taking Care of the Caregivers

Teachers do this work. They invent incredibly beautiful and important pedagogies, community practices, rituals, and memories. I have found that teachers struggle hard to "hold it together," to be there for the kids, while they become—if not the orchestrators, at least the conductors of the days and weeks that follow the death of a student. Many report that they feel numb, rather dopey, after some time. After all, while they are helping people let emotions out, they are holding them in.

In many religious traditions, the designated convener of a memorial or funeral is someone who often does not even know the deceased well. The family and friends can be present and able to deeply mourn while the priest, rabbi, imam, or other leader of the service simply moves the ritual forward. When students die in your class, however, no such separation exists. Teachers uncomfortably wear both hats—officiate and mourner.

While they are helping people let emotions out, they are holding them in.

After the initial struggle that the teacher takes on, there is often a period of collapse—who will take care of the caregivers? I watched Hasmig Minassian offer an answer to this dilemma when her students crowded into her house the night after two students were killed in an auto accident in Richmond. While she shared hugs and tea, while she allowed everyone to speak, she actually did not just hold it together. She took her own turn in the circle and expressed her own pain and horror. She managed to balance a genuine expression of her own suffering with her role as the adult in the room. She said later that she knew she could not go all the way into how desperately distressed she was—that could leave kids afraid, like there was no anchor and no safe port. However, she did not have to simply be strong—a stance that could in fact communicate that the best thing to do in this moment was to repress feelings.

Part of the answer is to stand somewhere between losing it and being the completely together leader. But more is needed. Teachers need another place, a space with colleagues and friends, to decompress, express, and just heal. I first learned this from LaShawn Routé. When Yaheem King was shot and killed, the African American Studies Department collapsed its walls in the B-Building and spent the day holding, listening to, and encouraging young people to reflect on and tell stories about this young man. At the school staff meeting that day, the principal began with the briefest mention of the incident and did not mention Yaheem's name, saying that we had to press on and move to an agenda item.

> **Part of the answer is to stand somewhere between losing it and being the completely together leader.**

I'll never forget LaShawn standing up at that faculty meeting and completely exposing her heart—asking faculty to understand that those who were teaching through tears were in need of indulgence, understanding. At the same time, she generously offered the faculty a lesson in humanity, in the complete humanity of Yaheem and all young Black men who were being killed regularly. She read to the faculty Nikki Giovanni's (1997) poem "All Eyez on U"—written on the occasion of Tupac Shakur's death. The poem is angry and polemical, but keeps returning to the soft, sweet line, "such a beautiful boy" (p. 62). LaShawn was holding all these roles, mourning, supporting, and leading. LaShawn was later called in to the superintendent's office and accused of being racially divisive. A vice principal scolded her saying that what she said was too strong.

Those teachers who are not as close to the student who has died need to take care of the caregivers. For some, this would be a night of drinks at a bar; for others it might be a walk in the hills; some need to go hear music; some will shelter at home. Whatever it is, teachers must be encouraged to do this part of the work. We have our own suffering, our own trauma. It has something to do with experiencing the death of a young person we love and with whom we are in an important relationship; but it also comes from seeing the suffering, being present for the suffering, of the students who are still here. Our trauma, however, is not ratified; it has no official place in the discourse of care and counseling; in a sense, it is a disenfranchised trauma. Yet the last thing a teacher wants to do is to demand the center of attention, to seem to be saying "What about me, me, me?" Teachers cry, even when there is not a major tragedy, and it is very important for students to witness their teachers as human, as it is important for them to see all adults in their lives as real, vulnerable, and caring individuals. Yet the general notion of the teacher's role is that there is "no room for whining."

> Our trauma, however, is not ratified; it has no official place in the discourse of care and counseling; in a sense, it is a disenfranchised trauma.

After the funeral of our beautiful and thoughtful young student, Canon Jones, a group of teachers zigzagged our way to Juan's Place, a Mexican restaurant and bar. Margaritas and sangrias flowed. Food was consumed. And a kind of loopy, goofy few hours ensued. It was not only sadness and mourning. A manic atmosphere showed up, odd jokes were barked, silly moments from the service were remembered, and then every once in a while a side talk about how this student or that one was holding up. The whole gathering had a feeling of unreality, with the bar and other diners fading into a one-dimensional gauzy background. We were decompressing, I suppose. But we were also healing, recharging, free-floating in feelings and fears, gathering our spirits to go back to the students again the next day.

Good teachers after only a few years become wise, become community leaders. The encounter with death, horrific and awful as it is, moves teachers to positions of elders. Akira Kurosawa addresses this wisdom in his film *Ikiru* (*To Live*) (1952):

> I realize what they say about the nobility of misfortune is true. Because misfortune teaches us the truth. Your cancer has opened your eyes to your own life. We humans are so careless. We only realize how beautiful life is when we chance upon death.

This is a knowledge we now have. Sometimes it is not a knowledge we even want to have, but it has been thrust upon us. It has become a given.

The greatest work in becoming a teacher, as only teachers understand, is the journey to self. It is the matter of uncovering and examining one's prejudices and privileges, one's passions and deepest values. Good teachers know that the person who came out of undergraduate studies is not really enough. Teaching requires self-knowledge while at the same time it is a practice of struggling to figure out and enact what is best for students, for the children of others. Deep study, deep experience is crucial—in both subject matter and in understanding young people. Making such a journey requires that a new teacher be vulnerable and courageous; she must be able to creatively innovate, going to new and unexplored places not only in the world but also in the human heart. And when a student dies, everything about that journey will be called upon, will be accessed, in service of the kids and in service of the teacher's own survival.

1/30. Bloodroot. After Tupac

Molly Raynor

Molly Raynor is young teacher educator with RAW Talent poetry program, Richmond, California.

Friday, April 19, 2013, at 12:57 A.M.

This morning I woke up and it was still true.
I walked around Berkeley, studying flowers,
Trying to remember their names.
Morning glory.
Forsythia.
Hibiscus.

All I can think is the one name on everyone's tongue.
Dimarea.
Dimarea.
Dimarea.
How many bullets in your head?
When your brain shut down, where did the poems go?

He turned your body vacant lot.
He turned the street beneath you garden.
Bougainvillea.
Bloodroot.
Poppy red.

Two weeks ago we visited a farm in Richmond.
The farmer told us when she tries to sell her vegetables
At the Marin farmer's market, people have questions.
Is it OK to eat plants that grew in Richmond?
I mean, you know, with the Chevron Refinery,
And of course all the shootings.
It just seems . . . unsafe for things to grow there.

I don't feel it's my right to cry.
So I cough. Your name lodged in my throat like
A dead poem. A Black boy. A thirsty plant.

When Donte and Deandre found out, they paced,
Refused to stay inside the building.

Needed the air, the sun, the curb,
So close to the edge.

In Richmond,
The 5 stages of grief are different.
You don't take flowers to the grave,
You uproot them. If you're a *real* man(child),
You take life.

We women made a fence around their bodies,
Tried to pull them back into the building.
Never seen faces break like that,
Stems so solid snap like bone.

The funeral is tomorrow morning,
The slam is tomorrow night.
Trying to write poems after death,
Like trying to grow flowers in cement.
Still, they grow. Without fertilizer,
Without water, unsafe but still.
They grow, out of stoops and dumpsters,
Bust through cracks and corners towards light.

The ones who make it wear the brightest colors,
Have the boldest names,
Honeysuckle.
Petunia.
Violet.
Swirling their necks and singing to the sun.
I've always loved the wild ones most.

Dimarea.
Dimarea.
Dimarea.
Sounds like Donte.

Like Deandre.
Like the news that could
Shut me down for good.
So close, this time.
So close.

The plant on my desk is brown as your skin was.
Feel like I can't keep anything alive.

4. Wrong Steps

On the 1-year anniversary of Meleia's death, we held a meeting of
the main friends, allies, family just to check in. We decided to ask the
local mental health agency to send someone over, just to sit with our
circle, to offer any help or advice. Our meeting, after some hugs and
sad smiles, was simply a matter of sitting in a circle, each of us sharing
where we were at, what was going on. Some, especially those who had
been with Meleia when she died, were still raw and suffering. It was a
circle of tears, recriminations, guilt—everything. And it was good.

When the mental health intern spoke, she launched into a long
explanation of Elisabeth Kübler-Ross' "five stages of grieving." You
probably are familiar with this: denial, anger, bargaining, depression,
and finally acceptance. A hint to counselors: This might be a helpful
template for thinking about different types of grief, but it is not appropriate to say to the people who are grieving. It is simple-minded
in this moment, impersonal and schematic. Instead of helping people
in the circle, who were variously in tears and staring off into space,
this recitation only made them confused and angry. This was our time,
our emotions, our dear friend gone forever, not some predictable and
meaningless textbook case. Sometimes, I feel, our own anger and
nonacceptance were more real, more helpful, than the simplistic balm
too often offered. The people in the circle did their best to ignore the
intern's little talk and move on.

Anyone who has experienced a death in the family knows
the many wrong steps that people around them take in trying

to be comforting. When my mother died, we got a lot of them. The woman at the front desk at her care facility, who did not know us, opined, "She's in the arms of God now; she's a beautiful young woman, in no pain." I just looked at her in shock, too disgusted to even try to argue and not really wanting to upset her fantasy. I just wanted to get away from this crazy person. Although this may help some people, it is a jarring intervention to me and so many others.

And there are so many other ways to get it wrong, including:

- The advice that "God does not give us burdens we cannot handle."
- The advice that "You are being tested."
- Actually, any advice.
- Anything that attempts to give a social analysis during that first week. It may be on point, but it is just not the time.

It is important to simply be with the bereaved, to be attentive and supportive.

There are other wrong turns and mistakes. One common problem is the euphemism. What do you really say? *She died? She's dead.* It's almost too horrible to say. But then, *he passed on, passed away?* Not helpful. I remember when my mother was fading into the fog of Alzheimer's. We all tiptoed around the phenomenon. We did not want to say it. My brother Bill was most forthright and it was a relief. The family was going out to dinner with my parents one evening and we ran into some of their old friends. My mother was being odd and inappropriate. While we hurried to get her away, Bill said to the friends, "She's got Alzheimer's, so she's not really herself." They nodded and thanked us and everyone, including my mother, seemed relieved. *Alzheimer's. Death.* Say it. It's usually painful but it's for the best.

Whenever someone dies young, everyone who knows that person wonders, "What could I have done? How could I have stopped it?" Or even, "It's my fault." Teachers feel this, too. This includes questions of long-term steps one could have taken, things taught wrongly, and so on. And it sometimes includes immediate steps: "If only I had . . ." the day or the week of the incident. When Meleia died, I was haunted by memories of our teaching and discussions in senior seminar about standing up against injustice: Don't perpetrate injustice; don't be a bystander. Stand up, step in. So when the football players were sexually harassing these young women at 2:00 A.M., Meleia got in their faces. "You wouldn't appreciate someone talking to your mom like that! Or your sister!" She phoned friends to come help her. And they, too, heeding the lesson of being an upstander, came to help. Lots of wrong choices. Alcohol on all sides. But still, the feeling crept in. What did we teach them?

I have since come to my senses, realized that this was no more my fault, down in Mexico 2,000 miles away, than it was Denise's, who was standing right there. But I have added something to that classroom discussion of social ethics. I remind students that the call to be an upstander does not mean jumping in, Batman-style, to save the day. It means taking a stance every day, in small and large ways, against injustice.

For teenagers, also, there is sometimes a problem of the dramatic, the heart-rending aspect of death elevating it to something more important than other things in student life. By that I mean that death becomes romanticized or that teens romanticize themselves in it (thinking: "My life is more meaningful now that a friend died"). This had a very sad twist when there was a series of suicides at a railway site in Palo Alto. The notoriety of the last deaths inspired new students to commit suicide as well.

And then there is the phenomenon—appalling when you first realize it but really understandable—of some students seeking to get a social bump from being friends with the deceased. Some will even exaggerate their relationship for the sake of this bump. Adults can get angry at this but we have to remember that teenagers are in many ways adults and in other ways still children. That crazy mixture makes for bad judgment.

And the desperation for acceptance or status is nothing to be scoffed at. So be gentle with those who make such claims.

One other thought in the category of wrong steps: Quite often among the survivors some beautiful things are created; some hope for hope; some redemption. People tend to grope their way toward this and in a strange way it is beautiful. But then again sometimes it is not. We also know that there are cases where kids are not supported or do not find a way to come together. I know one case in which everything just got worse after a death, a funeral that was a nightmare. What can go wrong? Families fall out or fight; fingers are pointed; preachers take over the ceremony to speak too long and try to recruit new members; retaliation is threatened. Emotions are raw and the good stuff does not just come on its own.

Sometimes the school culture is not supportive of community building; sometimes the administration actually forbids teachers and classes to talk about the tragedy; sometimes we have failed to build the kind of trust that is a prerequisite for deep response. And we realize it is too late to start now.

> Quite often among the survivors some beautiful things are created; some hope for hope; some redemption. People tend to grope their way toward this and in a strange way it is beautiful. But then again sometimes it is not.

The best a teacher can do in all these circumstances is to find allies, colleagues and friends with whom to collaborate, to make plans to support the students. Sometimes the only thing is to bear witness, do your best to be present and helpful, and advocate strongly when you know the kids need it and no one else is stepping up. The whole experience requires tremendous courage.

Notes on a Classroom Responding to the Death of a Student

Jaimie Stevenson

Sometimes, often even, the administration does not believe that teachers should help students process the death of a student. Jaimie Stevenson, a student teacher in Philadelphia, Pennsylvania, reflects on the ways a teacher must sometimes subvert the orders from above in the interest of the students.

During my year-long student teaching placement in a large Philadelphia high school, I was disturbed to find our administration face the death of a student with silence. No full-school announcements, no assemblies, no moment of silence. An email from the principal to the staff read in its entirety: "Regretfully, we report the passing of Senior [name omitted] who was killed in an automobile accident over the weekend. Our counselors will be available for all students and staff." No guidance to teachers—many of whom replicated the silence in their classrooms—about how to respond. Subsequent incidents at the school—including the quieter death of a second student and the arrest of a school administrator for the sexual assault of a then-current student—proved that silence was the leadership's *modus operandi* for addressing complex issues with the school community.

When I searched for explanations among veteran staff, I learned that the previous year, a teacher's suicide had been treated similarly. To me, this pattern showed negligence to the role of school as a learning environment, where students can experience academic as well as emotional growth. It showed students that their school is not a place where they can arrive with their own questions about death, and that the inroads for support at school are prohibitively vague and unnavigable.

When I was a student, my own high school had failed similarly when it made it clear that it was disinterested in the suicidality and imminent death of one of my parents, despite the fact that I lived with this person and was their primary caretaker. Schools should be deeply invested in making sure that students are able to address the deaths in—and out—of school, which are bound to affect students' capacity to learn well, interact healthily with others, and cope. As a new teacher, it was distressing to find myself relying on a sense of emotional responsibility to initiate a conversation with my students about this instance of death, rather than work within any mechanism the school could have put in place to ensure that all teachers show their students that it is okay to talk about death publicly, and how.

Was the silence of the administration at this school a deliberate approach or was it the oversight of a large, hectic school with too few resources? Were administrators afraid of students' emotions? Were the school's leaders uncertain what their role should be, or how to advise teachers? Were they distrustful of students who might manipulate the death as an excuse to disengage from academic work? At the front of my mind was a healthier example from my own public elementary school principal, who responded to the school-year death of my 1st-grade teacher (she died from an undiagnosed brain tumor in her early 20s) by modeling a communal grieving and healing process that now seemed unusually caring for an institution. Was one caring leader responsible for the difference between the responses of my elementary school and this high school to a death in our school community?

My students were quicker to point out the silence than was I. At the end of the first school day after the student's death, I overheard a student in my last-period class talking about the student's death during a transition in the lesson. He told his group mates that he "could not believe" that he had gone through "an entire day" without a single teacher mentioning the death. I stopped the class when I heard his comment, and asked the whole class whether or not they had talked about it at all in their previous classes.

I did not disagree with the student—it was strange that an administrator had not made an announcement or called for a moment of silence, and I had not heard teachers talking with students about it either. Some students responded that one or two of their teachers had mentioned it or held a moment of silence in their own classrooms, but many students said that no adult had brought it up. So I improvised. I asked students to take out a sheet of paper for a free-write.

My prompt: "How do you want teachers and administrators to talk about the death of a student?" I told the class that this would not be a part of their grade; it was simply a way to help me understand what they needed in this moment. They could write anonymously.

Students' responses were fantastically honest, and fell on a wide spectrum of interpretations. The next morning, I provided the same prompt to my first-period class. Across the classes, students didn't agree with one another but many of them wanted much more than to ignore the situation. In response to students' writing in both classes, I held a 2-minute moment of silence at the end of each period.

In my mind, this wasn't anywhere near enough—I was embarrassed by the silence. The school's silence put my students in the position of *being the adult*—they had to *ask* for what they needed. My stomach clenches at the thought of the messages that the school sent in that moment: that it's okay to avoid talking about death, that it's not okay to talk about death at all, that the cause of a student's death mediates its impact, that we should care less about a student whose cause of death might have been wrapped up in underage drinking, or simply that if a school is large enough (in this case 3,000 students), then a student can disappear, or die, without mention. Of course, our schools replicate the habits of our society, which is undeniably shifty on the topic of death; but we need to resist schools' replication of this cowardly habit.

Student responses:

- "Honestly, I found it highly disrespectful that not ONE teacher said anything. It doesn't matter how this happened. Families and friends are GRIEVING and you run around like it's *nothing*."
- "I think that teachers should care about the students that have problems and issues. What they might do is talk to the adults of the student's family to know what's going on."
- "I don't feel anything. I don't like talking about death or funeral [*sic*] or anything in that matter."
- "The teachers should talk about it if they feel it is necessary."
- "In my opinion some teachers did not have her as a student, so it might be different. Although it is very upsetting and I am sorry for her, I do not think teachers should talk about it."
- "Teachers could make a group after school to talk about it. After all school is school."
- "I don't really CARE IF TEACHERS TALK ABOUT IT. It don't MAKE A DIFFERENCE."

- "I believe teachers should talk about it to get the point out there that death is serious. But to show respect maybe take a little time out to talk about it, but others may be hurt about the situation, and might not want to hear."
- "Moment of quiet then LEAVE IT."
- "If a student died I would want teachers just to respect the student and show some sympathy. An example on how to act during that time."
- "I would want teachers to stop ignoring the fact and acting like it didn't happen whether we knew the person or not we should still pay our respect because the student was a part of our [school] family."
- "LEAVE IT ALONE."
- "I think that the teachers should just take it slow. Because people that know the person are still grieving so there is still a lot of emotions. So they should just take it one step at a time."
- "I recommend that they say nothing the only person that should say something is the loud speaker and then there should be an assembly for each grade for clearance/clarity."
- "We shouldn't ignore it. We should be able to show our respects in our own way like the students who wore pink T-shirts today. A moment of silence and a simple nice talk about how everyone's affected by the death."

5. White Teacher

Here is a chapter that is not for everyone reading this. Because many of you are African American or Chicano/Latino/a or Asian American or Native American or Pacific Islander or members of other marked and marginalized groups. However, I can't explore student death without noting and coming to terms with my own identity. Being White in urban schools—and "urban" has come to be the euphemism for low-income Black and Brown, working-class communities—I come from more privilege. And, truth be told, almost all teachers have some privilege, either from birth or from ascension into the middle class. The educational system that got them here filtered out those who could not bow before the master narrative, the worldview, and the values of those in power. They had to either buy this package or at least pretend and fake it. I should add that this chapter could be called "White, straight male teacher" because the same caveats could be rehearsed with respect to gender and gender orientation.

Those of us who teach in oppressed communities, in working-class and colonized and marginalized communities, learn to implement culturally relevant teaching. Instead of assuming that our way of seeing the world, our way of speaking and writing and thinking, is the only way—we recognize that good teaching means understanding the strength of student cultures, the literacy and cognitive assets that students bring to the classroom. Education is not simply "come to me" but rather "let's take this journey together." And culturally relevant teaching does not mean making stereotyped assumptions about the values and practices of the students in front of us ("Here's an African American student, he must like hip-hop!"), but simply being attuned to, aware of, and respectful of the realities and practices of the students in front of us. If we aren't interested in student life, why did we become teachers? As an old White man, I would never attempt to act within the culture of the students, but I always show my enthusiasm and interest in their reality. And that works. Students are for the most part generous and welcoming if they sense respect and interest instead of othering and revulsion.

Nevertheless, I realize that my solutions, my insights, my perspectives are deeply colored by my middle-class status and my privilege. I can't help it, but I can be aware of it. When a 10th-grade student of mine, Lisandra, was caught up in Norteño gang posturing, half into being an awesome student and half jumping other girls to prove her mettle, when she was locked up in juvenile hall, I could only think: How can we get her out of here? How to get her far away, someplace new, with no gangs and no danger? What I was really dreaming of was how to get her to the suburbs. Silly, I know, but the fear—the constant and daily fear— was something I could not imagine her living in forever.

> As an old White man, I would never attempt to act within the culture of the students, but I always show my enthusiasm and interest in their reality. And that works. Students are for the most part generous and welcoming if they sense respect and interest instead of othering and revulsion.

When 15-year-old Jubrille was shot and killed in East Oakland in December, I wondered about my last encounters with her. Looking back on our small interactions as I supervised her student teacher, I couldn't help having that feeling again of wishing I had known then what would happen in the next month. What would I have done? Shout at Jubrille, "Don't worry about this damn essay. Get up! Run! Move somewhere, go somewhere, hitchhike across the country, run, run, run!"

And of course, this is simply the reflexive response that comes with my petty bourgeois framework. Lacking an idea of how to transform the cities, or imagining that such transformation would take a lot of time, I only wanted to help students escape. I only wanted to perform some kind of rescue. When I listened recently to Dave Stovall describe how he responded and moved with a student who was caught up and in danger, it revealed to me this deficiency of my perspective. For all my commitment to urban teaching and families, I was still seeing the community through a deficit lens, and I still saw escape as the only (however unrealistic) option.

I pause when I think that any assessment of the situation is so deeply grounded in my own middle-class and White world of privilege. I walk my dog every day, morning and night, in Oakland and basically feel no fear. Because I'm in that "other" Oakland; still the flatlands, but behind its own invisible walls. I'm in a safer part of Oakland, not the Deep East or the West Side. My imagination could not grasp much more than an escape fantasy for Jubrille. But "save one kid" is no strategy. We need the courage and vision to talk about transformation of the whole thing, to address the conditions that make this happen.

It's a dilemma. I'm the adult in their lives, sometimes a very important adult, and I have to offer insight and advice as an elder. Yet, it is important not to be seduced by the power of position, not to think that my idea of what to do is simply right. Indeed, we do a disservice to students if we lead them to believe that we have all the answers or even that we expect them to think that we have all the answers. We are facilitators, not gods. Knowledge is never autonomous and context-free. What we know is conditioned by our social position. Some wonderful things happen when we, people from very different worlds, parallel universes, encounter one another. But it is also easy to misjudge,

> "Save one kid" is no strategy; we need the courage and vision to talk about transformation of the whole thing, to address the conditions that make this happen.

to overstep one's expertise or even one's right to proffer advice. It is humbling. Or it should be.

How many of us have heard hip-hop songs that contemplate death, either their own or that of a loved one? Young people sing about the strong possibility that a boyfriend will be shot down and killed before the couple can really make a life together. As culture has always done, such songs help us understand the world we live in.

Wow. Do teenagers really have to think like this? Do they have to live this? Sure, we had the Shangri-Las' "Leader of the Pack," the song about the kid who dies in the car race in the 1960s. But now there are songs about something commonplace, the killing of young Black men. I have seen videos such as the scene in an ER, with heart paddles jolting the dying body of a boyfriend. The funeral home near my house regularly has large gatherings, spilling out onto the sidewalk, of Oakland youths bidding farewell to their peers.

This is what we White teachers have a blind spot against. The Justice Department estimates that 1 out of every 21 young Black men will be murdered, a death rate double that of U.S. soldiers in World War II. This is a horrible statistic. But compare this with our responses to death during World War II. There was a whole country, a whole culture, that was directed toward supporting the families, toward honoring the suffering. The songs, the movies, the presidential speeches, all gave tribute to those who lost their lives and those who had to carry on.

But these youngsters are dying, being cut down, really, with no acknowledgment, no validation even of their humanity. If hundreds of White people were killed each year in the city, the 82nd Airborne would be called in. Apparently, with African American youth dying, that problem is just their thing.

The point is, though, that we have no idea. We are clueless. We don't know what these young people are experiencing. And we are certainly not part of the solution—in helping them cope, helping them make sense of it, or helping to change the circumstances.

So, they create their own culture. They write hip-hop. They write rhythm 'n' blues. They write slams. They make their own sense of it. Is it our job, we White liberal teachers, to step in and "tut tut" over what they have gotten wrong? Do we understand, even a little, what is going on? This is a culture that has been abandoned—no, treated with contempt—by White people from the beginning. Oh, we love jazz now but we hated it then, when it was expressing African American insights.

What's the answer? I don't know. A little humility would help for a start. A little understanding of the real world in front of our faces. Even a little outrage. Instead of patronizing African American youth, instead of viewing them as deficits, we need to recognize the heroism of survival and resistance reflected in their culture. Perhaps then we can begin to take real steps that will stop the war (the one at home).

Finally, imagine a world in which the actual discourse, the actual creative culture of African American youth, was honored and elevated as the most creative, cutting-edge insight of our era.

I realize that I don't really understand the drug economy, the kinds of defeats of social movements that made communities turn on themselves. I can't fathom the horrors of the drug war in Mexico that has seen the murders of perhaps 60,000 people in the past several years. I am worlds away from the wholesale slaughter taking place in cities like Rio de Janeiro in Brazil. Teachers must be humble before the communities they are serving. We must not assume that our worldview is by default right and correct. We do not live in these conditions and we can easily succumb to a patronizing analysis of these students, a pathologizing of poverty. The default position, the notion that I know what is right for them, is generally one not to trust.

In his memoir, Ta-Nehisi Coates (2008) chastises us for these very assumptions and I can't help feeling implicated in his criticism and his anger:

Nowadays, I cut on the tube and see the dumbfounded looks, when over some minor violation of name and respect, a black boy is found leaking on the street. The anchors shake their heads. The activists give their stupid speeches, praising mythical days when all disputes were handled down at Ray's Gym. Politicians step up to the mic, claim the young have gone mad, their brains infected, and turned superpredator. Fuck you all who've ever spoken so foolishly, who've opened your mouths like we don't know what this is. We have read the books you own, the scorecards you keep—done the math and emerged prophetic. We know how we will die—with cousins in double murder suicides, in wars that are mere theory to you, convalescing in hospitals, slowly choked out by angina and cholesterol. We are the walking lowest rung, and all that stands between us and beast, between us and the local zoo, is respect, the respect you take as natural as sugar and shit. We know what we are, that we walk like we are not long for this world, that this world has never longed for us. (p. 177)

This makes me think about an experience I had in the 1980s. I was supporting an action by Black community housing activists, a tent city they had set up for the homeless in a downtown Oakland park. Our job was to be there, as witness, in case the police came. I slept there a number of nights. Sometimes I did observe police brutality and arrests; other times it was just a matter of sleeping. But lying on the ground, feeling the coldness seep up from the soil, hearing and seeing rats scurry around, I had an "aha" moment; or perhaps it was a "duh" moment. I realized that, of course, no one wants to be homeless. Well-sheltered people sometimes imagine that homeless people, some of them, simply have dropped out and have chosen to be homeless. Maybe they are mentally disturbed and want to stay outside. We don't think this consciously but many of us actually harbor such thoughts subconsciously. Lying there, trying to get some sleep, I was reminded that no, no one wants to live like this. No one. No one likes rats sleeping with them. You only get that understanding by sleeping there, not from a book or a discussion.

And with these young people I have to remind myself that no one wants to live in a drug and crime economy. No one. It

is not a choice. It's a world into which they are born. I'm reminded of the words of Easy Nofemela, a South African youth
convicted of killing American exchange student Amy Biehl during the apartheid period: "Killing someone like her exposed
both our anger and the conditions under which we lived. If
we had been living reasonably, we would not have killed her."
Today, the poor and colonized communities are not living reasonably. They live in a community stripped of resources and
jobs—this is the only economy many oppressed people are allowed into. So moralizing or criticizing or imposing my values
and my world on urban youth does not help anyone.

Does this mean there is some clear, some super-down,
some appropriate way to respond to the situation? Not at all. It
just means I have to put my own assumptions in check, even
my assumptions about what these young people need.

I was reminded of this truth by
Julie Daniels, who has taught English for the past 3 years at Fremont
High School in Oakland. Through
her own shock and sadness the
day after a student was killed over
the weekend, she asked the students what they wanted to do,
what steps to take. Nothing, they
replied, let's just do school. They
had seen so much death, they
were so beaten down with it, that
they did not want to wallow in its reality, did not want to
open up their deepest fears. For these students, the safest and
best immediate step was to "do school" for the day. She was
attuned to her students to such an extent that she agreed not
to do ritual, reflection, healing activities. She was in touch
enough to leave it at that. Because, she told me, it wouldn't
do for the teacher to force a process on the students just for
her own needs or her own sense of what was appropriate.
That itself could just be a middle-class performance. These

> Does this mean there is
> some clear, some super-
> down, some appropriate way
> to respond to the situation?
> Not at all. It just means I
> have to put my own assump-
> tions in check, even my as-
> sumptions about what these
> young people need.

students were hardened, but very soft at the same time. They just knew that, for now, for this day, they did not want to get into the death story.

So that reminds me again: There is no right answer. It might be in reenacting rituals and traditions; it might be in doing school as usual. The key to this, like the key to culturally relevant teaching, is to listen, to pay attention, and to respect the needs and knowledge of the young people.

6. Good Guys, Bad Guys

When we got back from Mexico, I called Bill Pratt to find out what was going on with the students, how all were coping, and what needed to be done for Meleia's memorial. "It's bad, Rick," he said. "And it gets worse. Are you sitting down?" I was sitting down, in a car. "She was not shot in a random event. It was friends. Charles and Titus have turned themselves in. The third, Santana, who was apparently the shooter, is wanted."

It was a sudden, second incomprehensible blow: Meleia has been shot by our former student and her good friend Santana, and the car that brought him to the scene had other former students in it as well. Meleia had called Santana when she and some other young women were being sexually harassed by Cal football players out late on a summer evening of partying. Santana hadn't meant to shoot her, and in fact had come to help, but he had brought a gun and that was the end of it.

What the hell? I had constructed the shooter in my mind as some "other," some anonymous gangster from Richmond or something. But it wasn't true—our student had shot our student; the wonderful Meleia was dead at the hand of the amazing Santana. What a nightmare. I had thundered to a friend, "Who was this young man's teacher?!" Now it turned out that I was the teacher. That's the Greek side of the tragedy, the "don't point your finger, look to your own house."

When we lose a loved one, particularly to violence, we have a great need to canonize her, to declare her an innocent saint who never did anything wrong, who died at the hands of an evil person, a devil.

Meleia's friends were right on the main point—she was a delightful, caring, self-sacrificing, radical leader. When this group of jocks came upon a group of young women out for the evening, they approached aggressively. When Meleia and her friends declined interest, the young men became abusive, calling them bitches, Chewbacca, and more. Although the other young women wanted to get in the car, let it go, just leave, Meleia wanted to correct them. "You wouldn't call your mother that. You wouldn't call your sister that. What makes you think . . ." and so on. Outnumbered and feeling threatened, she phoned Santana, who was at a nearby party—come help me, come back me up. The question, the contention, is whether she told Santana to "bring the heat" or bring the gun, as some claimed to have heard. Some said she did not know Santana had a gun. Some argued that she was appalled by violence and would never suggest such a thing. There was no doubt that Santana had done something terrible, horrible, and most supremely stupid. But what was the whole story? It was impossible to tell.

I'm not trying to write an analysis of violence in America here; I'm really not. The problem of a shattered economy, of populations deemed surplus and expendable, of Black on Black and Brown on Brown crime, of the drug economy and police as an occupying force instead of community upholders—all of these would have to be unpacked. It is almost inconceivable to look at places like Harper High School in Chicago where 29 students were killed in a single year. The NPR radio program *This American Life* did an extensive and painful profile of the Harper killings of 2012 (http://www.thisamericanlife.org/radio-archives/episode/487/harper-high-school-part-one). But too often, the killings go on anonymously, behind the screen of invisibility that is the American racial blind spot.

And we must acknowledge that too often authority figures also shoot our young people, whether it is Oscar Grant shot by Oakland transit police or Michael Brown shot by a Ferguson police officer. This is one reason young people feel alone, with no security force that is theirs, that they can turn to. But that analysis belongs in another book, probably a much longer one written by someone who understands much more than I do.

But we look out on our classroom and worry—who might be killed next? And, even more horrifying, who might be the next one who kills?

My sister-in-law Bernardine Dohrn has done crucial and important work on juvenile justice and the criminalization of youth. When she came to speak to my education class on adolescents, I asked her how she explained those young people who kill their peers. I was still trying to sort out the good guy/bad guy binary, to explain how a young person turns to something so horrible.

> **But we look out on our classroom and worry—who might be killed next? And, even more horrifying, who might be the next one who kills?**

Her response was not simple or assured but it made me wonder more. She explained that in a community where economic options are virtually nonexistent, where any young person might be induced to "post up" on this corner or that corner, to play a small role, it is never a simple story. Add to that the easy availability of lethal weapons, guns in the hands of youth often too young to even calculate or imagine the chain of consequences of their actions, and tragedy is bound to happen. Imagine a Black mother opening her door to the knock of a police officer early in the morning, she said. This mother does not know if she will learn that her son has been shot or has been arrested as a shooter. In either case, her world and the world of so many others will be devastated.

Although we believe in personal responsibility, people are also a product of their environment. In a community with no viable economy, with no safety in the face of authority, with few ways to live, people make their own assessment of the world, build their own culture to cope with that world. As Gwendolyn Brooks (1994) writes:

I shall create! If not a note, a hole.
If not an overture, a desecration.

She is pointing out that the youth say they will make a noise—if not positive, then destruction. If we are there for our students, if we have a kind of educational unconditional love, then we must find a way to be there for them also when they create a desecration. I think about the moment in Lorraine Hansberry's (1959) *A Raisin in the Sun* that knocks me out. It is when the son Walter Lee Younger has spent the family savings that were going to go toward finally buying a house. When Walter Lee's mother says we still need to love him, his sister Beneatha Younger is furious and declares, "Love him? There is nothing left to love." And the mother replies:

> There is always something left to love. And if you ain't learned that, you ain't learned nothing. (Looking at her) Have you cried for that boy today? I don't mean for yourself and for the family 'cause we lost the money. I mean for him: what he been through and what it done to him. Child, when do you think is the time to love somebody the most? When they done good and made things easy for everybody? Well then, you ain't through learning—because that ain't the time at all. It's when he's at his lowest and can't believe in hisself 'cause the world done whipped him so! When you starts measuring somebody, measure him right, child, measure him right. Make sure you done taken into account what hills and valleys he come through before he got to wherever he is. (p. 113)

Yes, that is some hard love. And it is quite different from liberal permissiveness, from sentimental or romanticized forgiveness. It means being as sharp as possible about proper action, how to move, what to say.

But just as any mother has to worry and wonder about the danger her child is in, teachers find ourselves worrying not only if our kids will be injured and killed but also whether our own students will commit the unspeakable crime. We don't have very good methods, as a society, to deal with such developments. And again teachers are not given guidance, suggestions, or insights on what to do in such a case. It is easy enough to simply eject the perpetrator from one's world from afar. The toxic, anonymous comments, the so-called troll comments that appear after newspaper stories online reflect a frightening collective unconscious, the hegemonic consensus, in our society. "Good thing a thug killed a thug. Saves the court costs." "Lock 'em up and throw away the key." "What's wrong with the parents who raised these kids?" And then there's the semi-official endorsement of rape: "I hope he's ready to become someone's wifey for the next 30 years." Hair-raising and racist comments remind us how far we have to go.

But if he's our student, if he's my student, we know better. We know the human tragedy here. What should be done? One thing we know is that this perpetrator is not going to disappear. He will have a life, some kind of life, in prison. He will come back into society. We will encounter him on the street. Will he be unable to find his way in the world? Will we meet him at the end of a stick-up gun? Or will he be one of those broken spirits begging for some quarters in the business district? Is there another way?

And everyone in this situation, everyone in this world, suffers. A young teacher wrote to me, "At least five of the students in my creative writing class have an immediate family member that has been murdered within the last 3 months. How do I serve them effectively? I am so scared to let them down; I am so scared that I will fail them." It has been estimated that youth in our cities are suffering from PTSD (posttraumatic stress disorder) two times more frequently than soldiers in Iraq, yet it is not "post"; it is *permanent* traumatic stress syndrome. If we understand why some veterans go off in violent explosions, we must understand the same behavior in these youth. The work, for instance, of Jeff Duncan-Andrade (2009) and of Perry and Szalavitz (2006) demonstrates the ways that such trauma affects everything in a youth's life and is even passed down between generations. And once I had a name for it, I began to see this kind of psychological pattern throughout schools.

What is it like to grow up in constant danger? Tara Singh, one of Meleia's friends from high school, has now grown up and become a fantastic teacher. I went to visit her 3rd-grade class and sat in on sharing time.

In halting but matter-of-fact language a child named Marisol starts her story: "One day my mom and I were home. There was a man outside yelling. He was a neighbor. We went out to see what was happening. He didn't have a shirt on and he had a gun.

"Then another man came out and yelled at him, 'Why are you shouting for no reason?' And then the man with no shirt, he shotted him."

End of story. I was stunned but felt responsible to stay quiet, to stick with the class norms. Ms. Singh simply asked, "Are there any questions?"

> *Sean:* Where did he shoot him?
> *Marisol:* In the body. In the chest.
> *Ty:* Did you see it?
> *Marisol:* Yes.
> *Marisa:* What did you do?
> *Marisol:* Me and my mommy ran in the house.
> *Kevin:* Was he Mexican?
> *Marisol:* Who?
> *Kevin:* The guy with the gun.
> *Marisol:* Black.
> And that was that.

I wondered what Tara would do next. Calm as could be, she asked, "What do you do when you are scared? How do you make yourself feel safe?"

Wow, I thought. What a genius move. No sense emoting about the horror of the experience, our outrage that kids this age need to experience it. This is their life; this is their world.

The place to take the conversation is forward. Not to imagine an end of violence altogether but perhaps to explore and share ways to cope, to survive.

What followed was a long list of responses to dangerous situations. Many of them had to do with hiding in closets, hiding under beds, turning off lights. One girl said she would watch TV. Some kids described seeking safety with an adult. For some, it was about being alone. But they all had ready answers. And they were smart and thoughtful and beautiful. And heartbreaking.

Afterward, Tara reflected that Marisol looked anxious when broaching the subject, fidgeted uncomfortably while telling her story. I had not seen that at all. She seemed fine, perhaps with a little stage fright. But of course that was because Tara knew these kids well, knew every gesture and tone of voice. She picked up the courage, and the need to share, that was behind Marisol's declaration. This was a teacher and a classroom community doing important work together.

This moment reminds us that children grow up with this kind of trauma, this kind of danger, their whole lives. That is not to say that peer death during high school is not a shock. Just that children have been prepared for it, awash in it, terrified of it, since they first opened their eyes and gazed upon the world into which they were born.

And it makes me sick. I want to address the challenges, heal the trauma, and all of that. But I can't believe this is what we are reduced to; that we are doing therapy and not really changing the fundamental conditions. We are not just working to mitigate trauma, we are struggling to provide critical hope, the understanding that there is work to be done that will change the conditions that produce trauma. We work in this context; we do awesome things in this context. But we should never be satisfied to tolerate this context. May we never get used to this.

The truth is that we must find another way to think about and act toward those who commit violent acts—not just because we want better outcomes, a more functional and harmonious society, but also because we have met this kid, and we know him not as a statistic or a perp. Instead, we know him as a person, one with hopes and dreams; one with a complex internal life and a deep psychological landscape; one who has suffered trauma and responded to circumstances that are not of his own making. If teaching is the building of relationships, the creation of community and tribes and posses and sets and circles, then it seems artificial and arbitrary that the relationship is severed at 3:30 when the bell rings or in June when school lets out. The obligations of community, to be there for the other, means to, at least sometimes, reach across the boundaries of official school time to connect to families and communities. At some times this means going to *quinceañeras* and weddings, to baby showers and funerals; at others it means visiting prison.

Although the trauma explanation is compelling, I would approach it as only one lens and one with limitations. Too often, it is reinterpreted by young teachers as a new version of the culture of poverty myth, but with a progressive veneer. In other words, we must take the debilitating effects of poverty and oppression very seriously. But we cannot stop there and treat young people from these communities as deficits or as psychologically scarred beyond repair. For the other side of the story is the resilience, the creativity, the powerful critical thinking that youth bring to their lives and to the classroom. Although the oppressed suffer psychological damage, the cure resides not simply in psychology (therapy or psych drugs). The solution lies in action in the world, action to improve circumstances, action to change society. This is where teachers and texts and curriculum and pedagogy come in—and they are crucial.

Every child needs a caring adult in his or her life, someone who allows them to see themselves more fully. That adult might be anyone— a mother, a father, an aunt or uncle, a probation officer, a caseworker, a

> Every child needs a caring adult in his or her life, someone who allows them to see themselves more fully. That adult might be anyone—a mother, a father, an aunt or uncle, a probation officer, a caseworker, a coworker, or a teacher.

coworker, or a teacher. Teachers are often the ones who have made that connection, even if you don't see evidence of it for years, or ever. Teachers go about their work with this compelling idea: I may be the one, in this encounter, who gives this kid a reason to hope. When youth are caught up in the system, sitting in prison, just a letter once in a while from an adult who thinks the youth is more than the worst thing he has done, a note that says, "You are someone; you matter," can make all the difference. Teachers send books inside and then ask their former students to read them, and tell us what they thought. And some teachers, sometimes, visit the prisons, make a link with the parents and family, and continue the relationship. This is not for fun or glory; it is because we must; we feel the obligation from the relationship we started with these kids so many years before.

My brother Bill talks about the year he taught in Cook County Juvenile Hall and the honor he had of getting to know Tobes, an elderly White man, an Irish Catholic ex-priest, who worked there for years. Tobes was unfazed and unafraid, encountering and supporting young people who had done horrible things, including murder. Although I don't share the same religion, I was always moved by his guiding ethic, his view that "all people, whatever they have done, are a reflection of, a piece of, God." To be in awe of the transcendent importance of this person, of the incalculable value of one life, is a guiding ethic that must underlie effective teaching. And it beckons to us when this young person has committed a small transgression or a large crime. When we understand the humanity of the young people caught up in the life, the options and choices they have and don't have, we must be humbled; we must check our easy moralizing.

I think of this as I read the stunning memoir *Men We Reaped* by Jesmyn Ward (2013), a story of five men in Ward's African American community in rural Mississippi who died too young:

> My hope is that learning something about our lives and the lives of the people in my community will mean that when I get to the

heart, when my marches forward through the past and backward from the present meet in the middle with my brother's death, I'll understand a bit better why this epidemic happened, about how the history of racism and economic inequality and lapsed public and personal responsibility festered and turned sour and spread here. Hopefully, I'll understand why my brother died while I live, and why I've been saddled with this rotten fucking story. (p. 19)

The simple truth of her narrative, and the explosion of anger at the end, perfectly captures the crisis and the horror of the circumstances young people from marginalized communities endure.

If we know the criminal justice system is wrong in the abstract—is ridiculously large and punitive and countereffective—then it is wrong in the particular, too. Hundreds of prisoners have been released when their convictions were found to have been fraudulently obtained. Thousands are serving time for drug offenses that would evoke a wink and slap on the hand at White-dominated college campuses. Thousands more do their hard time and come out determined to straighten things out in their lives. And most of the people who survive and come out able to function report that someone did connect with them—someone sent a book, wrote a letter, let them know that they were still human and still mattered in the universe.

In the weeks and months after Meleia's death, things certainly did not get easier. Two of the young men in the car had turned themselves in but the shooter, Santana, was on the run. Meleia's friends were anxious that the newspapers might "slander" her or sully her name. Any suggestion, which some had made, that she had called Santana and asked him to "bring the heat" was greeted with outcries and denunciations. We needed our saint and we needed our devil. When Santana was arrested 6 months later and went to trial, Meleia's behavior came up again. Would she be vilified or would we preserve her legacy as someone who fought for justice, who was appalled by violence? And at Santana's sentencing, the family and friends were split, some suggesting that Meleia would want clemency for her good friend who had done a terrible thing; some wishing him the longest possible sentence. Given the trends of California sentencing, Santana got the stiffest sentence possible in a case that was not an intentional murder—24 years.

Although I was still furious and disgusted with Santana, I was drawn to talk to him. I had to know his version, what was going on that night. And I wondered how Santana, someone who had huge challenges in his life and barely made it through high school, was looking at his life and prospects. Plus I was trying to support a reconciliation process, something between Santana and Meleia's family, which had started. So I did visit him, first in the Oakland lockup, and later at California prisons. During my first visit, he seemed scared and disoriented, uncertain even what he was doing day-to-day, confused about the appeal process on his sentence, which he told me "someone" was filing. I was afraid he would not be able to handle the harsh conditions of prison. The Santana I saw later in prison was harder, more physically buff, more certain of his movements, with even a deeper voice. He was more streetwise. I knew he could survive, but at what cost?

He described to me his anguish at what had happened. "I killed my best friend," he said, "and every day I think it would be best if I just died." At other times he was defiant, angry at those who had spoken against him. He insisted that she had called him for help. In his telling of it, he was at a party nearby, she called him and told him to come, to bring the gun. He was drunk and tried to beg off but she called again and again, insisting that he come. He got some friends to drive him. There was no way he was going to physically fight these guys so he intended to scatter them by shooting in the air with his cheap, Saturday night special gun. He jumped out of the car and from half a block away he fired some shots. Not knowing how to use the gun, not understanding the way a gun moves up and down as it backfires, he ended up shooting into the crowd and, incredibly, one bullet pierced right through Meleia's heart.

There is plenty of blame to go around for the fatal encounter that night in July 2005. For starters, some blame belongs to the football players whose sense of entitlement and sexual aggression had them roaming and harassing young women. The university quickly issued a statement that essentially said, "Our guys didn't do it; they are innocent; they committed no crimes; you can't prove anything." Anyone who knows big college football recognizes the disgusting institutional cover-up here. Oh, and the university donated $5,000 to the Meleia scholarship fund.

There was also blame on the other side. Meleia's friends felt they did not do enough to pull her back, to get her to disengage from the argument with the jocks. Everyone made bad choices. And most likely Meleia did not use the best judgment herself. One thing is clear: Everyone that night had been drinking.

Although we seek to make any tragedy a simple duality—the wonderful angel cut down by the terrible devil—reality is much messier. There is plenty of blame to go around. I realize now that it really does not matter whether Meleia was the entirely innocent victim who did nothing wrong or if she made bad or even terrible decisions. We would all like our last moment to be noble and clean. But everyone has their best and worst moments and decisions. The truth is that we would not love Meleia any less, we would not be any less devastated by her death, no matter what went down that night. There is no need to patrol and censor the accounts of what happened that night. Meleia's life, her whole life of caring and acting, is her legacy. Not what happened on that July night.

On Losing Students

Crystal Laura

Crystal T. Laura, PhD, teaches teachers and other school leaders at Chicago State University and is the author of *Being Bad*.

I lost my brother, Chris, when he was just a kid. Barely 18. Lanky with wide eyes like saucers. Funny, artistic, and sweet as pie. Chris had a world of possibilities ahead of him. Until January 2011. You see, at 18, Chris was arrested in connection with a slew of armed robberies he denies, and ever since he has been facing the ugly truth: A young Black man with five felony cases open and hanging overhead is done for. It kills me to admit it. He's 21 now—jobless, depressed, and looking to spend the next half a century behind bars. My brother is not dead, but he's not living, either.

What happened with Chris was a completely preventable tragedy. I can see that now with the kind of guilt-laden clarity and conjecture one can only have in hindsight. But I think it is still worth sharing my brother's story here in a book for teachers who love their students enough to deal with the grief of losing them, and who bothered to read another teacher's thoughts on doing so. This is Rick's book—not mine—so I will keep it brief.

Chris was the kind of student who could easily fall through the cracks of any big urban high school: smart as a whip—and bored out of his mind, disengaged, spotty in attendance. My brother's grades weren't remarkable. He wasn't an athlete, or a band geek, or otherwise active in any extracurricular programs that may have connected him to the school in some meaningful way. So when he stopped going altogether, in 2008, not a single school adult noticed, or if anyone did, nobody seemed to care.

No one called or stopped by my house to see what was up. Had my parents been asked, they would have likely shared the same tidbits I was recently told—that Chris had never quite properly healed from school wounds he'd sustained back in 4th grade, that his curiosity and bounding energy had been mistaken for an inability to sit still and think straight, that with repetition he'd learned to believe this, too. And that Chris had checked out of school long before he dropped out.

No one asked Chris where he thought he was going, except for the counselor who documented my brother's "transfer" to another educational institution, rather than calling it what it was and counting it as a loss—an awfully common and commonly understood practice to protect institutional interests by manipulating the numbers. Had someone expressed genuine concern, they'd have discovered that Chris was heading to the Job Corps, of all places, the U.S. Department of Labor's boarding school for "the bottom of our society." Not my words, of course; I lifted them from Chris Weeks, a political staffer who was on the ground floor of the Job Corps' origin back in the 1960s. Weeks (1967) wrote in *Job Corps:*

Dollars and Dropouts: The program was "focused on a specific prob-lem of undeniably critical proportions—masses of teen-agers who had been born into and raised in poverty, and who, because of this background, had little hope for earning a decent income or becom-ing productive citizens during their lives"—a problem that had long been complicated by weak government efforts to help. "To solve this problem," again, not my words, but Weeks'—"it seemed to have a promising formula for success—take these youngsters out of their ghetto tenements and rural shacks and put them in a clean, health-ful Job Corps center where massive injections of remedial educa-tion and job training would turn them into law-abiding, tax-paying good neighbors" (Weeks, 1967). Insulting, don't you think?

My brother had a different, benign, self-gratifying outlook on things. He was sold on the incentives that drew more than 300,000 applications from all across the country within 3 months of the pro-gram's inception and today pull in some 60,000 youth each year. In the Job Corps, Chris thought he could get a GED, three square meals per day, spending money, help finding work, and a small stipend to hold him over until his first paycheck came. He'd have ample spare time for sports and recreation, to pick up a trade, and to live away from home for the first time with people his own age. I had my reservations, but I suppose I can understand the allure: Whatever his everyday life was like in high school paled in comparison to the sexiness of the Job Corps.

Chris left school with pleasure but without a diploma in the funk of a recession, a time when basic necessities such as food and gas were more expensive than they had been in the past, homes were less valuable, big spenders had turned frugal, and dignified jobs paying living wages were hard to come by. I remember that moment especially because I was a broke doctoral student at the time, and I knew that even with an advanced degree, in a flooded market, my chances of finding a position were slim. So what a teenager would do with few skills and no credentials scared me to consider, and as commendable as Chris was for having a plan, his plan didn't allay my fear. Oh, how I wish there had been someone from the school—a teacher, a counselor, a dean, a principal, a superintendent—to say to Chris, (1) being in school is a lot safer for you than not, (2) you matter to me and to many other people here, and (3) we'll go to the depths to figure out why you want to leave and to keep you around.

I wonder if anyone from his school has thought of Chris or his whereabouts since he went missing in action. Do folks know that he graduated from the Job Corps to part-time work selling shoes, and within months, found himself in a maximum-security wing of Cook County jail? Probably not. If they did, I'd like to think that there'd be some serious soul-searching happening in the school. I'd hope that the devastating news would spread like wildfire and open up spaces for painful conversations about what happens, what to do, what it means, when students disappear. And then I'd want the school community to respond, or as Rick put it, to "enter the heartbreak of it and find a way to repair the gash in the social fabric." To fight and act like an overprotective family whose young lives depend on it.

A Letter

David Stovall

David Stovall is an associate professor of education at University of Illinois, Chicago.

Dear Rick,

In our uneven and often troubling moments of reflection, there is much to contend with as we come to grips with the fact that a member of our classroom community is no longer with us.

For myself, living in a city (Chicago) where community members are actively resisting decades of disinvestment, disenfranchisement, marginalization, and isolation, I am reminded of the complexities that may come with the death of a student. Where we feel the pain of the death internally, there are often external factors that are just as central to understanding how our students are sometimes caught in the crosshairs of intricate systems that play out in our neighborhoods. Often times the way these instances play out go under the radar. For myself, this is often heightened when a student dies violently. I pay special attention to this because we often focus on the tragedy of the loss of life and the instantaneous removal of someone from our classrooms.

Before reducing such losses to simple "gang-related" altercations or the actions of a few "bad apples," sometimes we need to take a step back. While this is often extremely difficult to do (especially in the immediacy of learning about the death) part of our healing may include understanding that our students' death is often connected to a larger and deeper reality.

Chicago provides a window to understand how these complex realities can play out in our lives as classroom teachers. In a hyper-segregated city ravaged by disinvestment (removal of resources) and the displacement of thousands of African American and Latino/a families over the last 20 years, conflicts are often exacerbated by city policies. This was most recently realized in the closure of 47 schools on the South and West sides of the city (both predominantly low-income/working-class African American neighborhoods), which is the largest single set of school closings in the history of the United States. Predating this round of school closures are the Chicago Housing Authority's (CHA) Plan for Transformation and Chicago Public Schools' (CPS) Renaissance 2010. Where the former was used to demolish over 90% of all high-rise public housing, the later was used to close existing schools and create an avenue for "new" schools (largely in the form of charter or contract schools). As public housing was razed, many families were forced out of the city. Those that remained had limited housing choices, often placing them in unfamiliar neighborhoods.

Because gang structures in Chicago are largely decentralized due to the drug trade, many large organizations have broken into fractions (cliques) that have little allegiance to the larger set (gang). These cliques operate on a "block-to-block" basis, as members are often more concerned with the underground economy. If someone new moves to one of these blocks, tensions may arise because of the previous neighborhood they come from, not necessarily because they're in a gang. In a city that's hyper-segregated, there is often little familiarity with other neighborhoods. These tensions are sometimes generations old and should be considered part of a larger divide-and-conquer strategy utilized by the city that pitted communities against each other for resources. We often dismiss this as an "inner-city" problem, but in most unmediated instances where significant numbers of people are placed in unfamiliar situations, conflicts arise. This can happen in cities, in affluent suburbs, and in rural areas. Instead of delving deep into this reality, it is easy to couch it as a city problem on the 20-second newsbyte on the nightly news.

Returning to the lives of our students, these undercurrents are difficult to realize when we're dealing with something as tragic as death by gun violence. At the same time, it should also be a realization of the idea that conflicts can be engineered by the state and passed off as individuals "acting badly." For myself, in the tragic event of a student's violent death, I have to push myself to understand that it's often deeper than what we may think.

In Struggle,
David Stovall, PhD
Volunteer Social Studies Teacher
Greater Lawndale High School for Social Justice
Associate Professor
University of Illinois, Chicago

7. Our Worst Nightmare

Mass shootings in schools grab the headlines and tap into our deepest fears. However, the truth is that school is a safer place for youths than the home. Although school shootings are horrendous and stand as a national nightmare in the media, the chances of a student being killed in school are one in two million. By comparison, according to the Justice Policy Institute, 16 children are killed by gunfire every 2 days in America, and 16 children die at the hands of their parents or guardians every 3 days in America.

Still, school shootings are on the rise. And there is no doubt that the vulnerability of children in school touches something primal and we wonder, deep in our hearts, what would we do? It turns out that in every case teachers throw themselves in front of their students, they lunge to get them out of the way, they move, unarmed, toward the person with the gun. This is not ever something they were trained for. Or rather, it is something we trained for every day in being responsible for students. It is just a reflexive response to the stance we carry every day.

> It turns out that in every case teachers throw themselves in front of their students, they lunge to get them out of the way, they move, unarmed, toward the person with the gun. This is not even something they were trained for. Or rather, it is something we trained for every day in being responsible for students.

All the teacher-bashing discussions about education seem to overlook this fact.

Perhaps a short section here will at least let us think of this unthinkable eventuality. I am going to report here an interview with my friend Dick Streedain. He was the principal of an elementary school in Winnetka, north of Chicago, in the late 1980s when mentally ill adult Laurie Dann walked in and started shooting students. That day stays with him even now, just as vivid as when it happened. Part of the account comes from a recorded interview. I leave in the way he jumps between the past and present tense because that is just how the memory works, when someone is trying to tell something that happened but then is suddenly back there and is speaking of it like it's happening now:

It hit us at a time when we were a healthy school community. We weren't fragmented. We have created a high degree of coherence in the curriculum. We started with class meetings.

It was a day when everything was blooming. It was May and it was all of a sudden spring. Warm day, the kids were having their bicycle test. I remember being on the playground before school watching the kids play. I was watching one kid who was a little shaky and I was hoping he was going to make it. And I remember seeing Nick Corwin and thinking, I don't have to watch Nick; he will do fine. And walking away. Another group of kids were going on a fieldtrip that day, so they were kind of getting ready. I have always loved the playground, lunchtime, before school. I'd always be out on the playground. It was just how I view the work.

I had brought in the best nurse I ever had. Her daughter had come to visit. She was this young, blond woman wearing all white. I was showing her around the school. It must've been around 10 o'clock or 10:30. We were walking around and having a great time. All of a sudden we heard (he snaps his fingers two times) some sounds. Then I heard a teacher running and saying there's been a shooting in the bathroom. As I'm walking down there, somebody else yells out, somebody's been shot in my classroom. So I run down there.

At that point in time, when I heard that there was a shooting I thought somebody had brought a BB gun. Something really crazy. A couple of weeks before a kid named José had done something in the bathroom and lost his bathroom privileges. So he had to pick out a classmate who could be trusted as his partner. So those two were in the bathroom together. Not doing anything wrong. Robert is another kid who happened to be in 1st grade. He had gone down to get some special support for reading. And he was in the bathroom, too. So all three of them were there. And that's when Laurie Dann popped in there. She shot Robert and went to shoot the other two but the gun didn't fire. So she leaves. I think she threw some ammunition in the sink. Robert managed to struggle down to the classroom. The other two kids went back to the classroom and said, "Mrs. Lind, there's been a shooting in the bathroom." Robert got to his room. So I went to his room. Then somebody else ran in and said there's been a shooting in the kindergarten. But that was a kid who'd been shot in the 2nd-grade classroom and had wandered down to the kinder-garten.

I walked into the classroom and I knew Nick was dead. The teacher wasn't there. She was gone. This happens so incredibly fast and then the kids saw me. The way the rooms are set up at Hubbard Woods, the classrooms have an outside door. A couple of kids were frozen but mostly they ran for the door. They ran to my office and hid behind my desk. I didn't tell them to do that. They just felt that the principal's office was the safest place in the school. So I ran with them. One of the kids said to me, Mr. Streedain, Lindsay isn't running so fast. I looked at her. It was like a ballpoint pen mark was on her; it wasn't red, but there was something there.

I said find out who's been shot and call their parents. And make sure both parents get called and let them know that something bad has happened. Everybody was very autonomous. They all play to their strengths. When the secretary was told the shooting started, she just started shaking. What do I do? And she thought, I'm just going to start ringing bells. The kids tell the story that when Laurie Dann started shooting, she would go boom, boom, boom. Then bells ring and she left.

You can't really plan for a tragedy like this. Who would say, ring the bells? Every time a kid came back, after the shooting, they had to replay the whole story.

Don Monroe, the superintendent of schools, and I are there. And the ambulances come and we hand over the kids. By now all the parents have been called. Within 15 or 20 minutes, every parent who came—somehow I was in a position to intercept them.

I remember walking down the hallway and thinking I'm the worst principal in the United States. Six kids got shot, I'm responsible for them, and I am a phony. There's no way I have the right stuff in me. I am like a chicken with his head cut off. Then suddenly, for some reason, a biblical admonition came to me, "The truth will set you free." Within the period of the minute, I crossed over a line from the most crazed I had ever felt to the most calm I had ever felt. It became very clear. I knew what I needed to do.

So that day, I get outside and Linda Corwin is walking down the street. Someone had called her. And she's looking at me, and she says, you better not have any bad news for me. And I kept on moving toward her and I said, "Linda, I've got the worst news a mother can ever hear. There's been a shooting in the school and Nick's been shot, and he's dead." And she just collapsed into my arms. And you know what she said to me? This is so remarkable. She said, "I feel the love around us here." Then she said, "I knew he was too good to last."

> Then suddenly, for some reason, a biblical admonition came to me, "The truth will set you free." Within the period of the minute, I crossed over a line from the most crazed I had ever felt to the most calm I had ever felt. It became very clear. I knew what I needed to do.

He truly was a beautiful kid. She said, "I've got to see him." I think, he's dead, there's blood all around, but how can I deny a mother? I said of course you need to see him. I walk her down to the room and just as we get there, the triage people had wrapped him up in like swaddling clothes. He was in a blanket and covered. She didn't see the torture to his body. I turn around and there's her rabbi.

That kind of thing just repeated itself throughout the day.

Our psychiatrist Mary Giffin went into the rooms with me when I told the kids that Nick was dead. The kids wanted to know the truth. Within about 20 minutes, the paramedics arrived and everything, and everybody's gone. The last thing I said to one of the triage guys, tell me what we've got here. He said, you've got one who we think isn't going to make it. But you got four others that I'm confident they'll make it."

As I walked in I was thinking about what I wanted to say. Mary Giffin was with me. And I just kept thinking, the truth will set you free. I realize you could tell kids anything. I said to the kids, "I wish I could spend all day with you, but I'll only be here about 5 minutes. I'm going to tell you the truth about everything that's going on. There are other adults here and I want to tell everybody the story at the same time. (There were a couple of moms who were volunteering at the school that day.) We've all had a day that we'll never forget for a lot of reasons." Now these kids had watched it. I said, "I want you to know how your classmates are. Robert was shot, but he is going to be okay. Tonight is going to be a critical night for Lindsey Fisher; they are not sure she's going to make it, but they are going to do everything they can to help her. And Nick. This is the hardest thing for me to tell you, but Nick has died." I remember they reacted like oh! Reality struck. Nick is dead! I said, "Right now what you need to do is use the adults in your room to talk about everything you saw and experienced. Draw or write or do whatever you need." Then I went to the next room.

Everybody seemed to know what to do. It just happened. A lot of social workers came over; ministers came over. Some of the rooms had 17 kids and 14 adults.

The next morning there were 900 people in the auditorium. I was not sad or nervous about it, though in a normal situation I would be. I can't understand that clarity. Whatever came, came. You didn't get to rehearse.

One of the most important ingredients for our ability to move through our school tragedy was a result of school culture that placed a high priority on teacher autonomy. On the day of the shooting this played out in numerous ways.

Teachers felt confident in their ability to make decisions based upon the needs of their children. Processing of the event was a natural extension of what was already in place to help children make sense of the daily challenges, hopes, and fears of their everyday experiences.

On the day of the shooting teachers were able to provide their students with experiences and activities that would help children process the tragedy through classroom meetings, conversations, drawings, block play, and drama. These activities would flow from the questions, concerns, and fears of the individual students as well as the collective community.

Teachers felt empowered to draw other available resources (volunteer parents, teacher assistants, student teachers, and auxiliary staff) into their classrooms to help work through the many immediate challenges as well as those during the remaining days of the school year.

Teachers felt comfortable to share how they planned to conduct classroom meetings the next day in their rooms. These meetings the following day included children, parents, and extended families. The task was to process the previous day's event and to lay the groundwork for what was ahead. Several teachers chose to go it alone. Several others wanted a close colleague to be with them. A few others asked to have a social worker, psychologist, or grief counselor help with or lead the parent and community conversations.

Teachers were given a notecard to explicitly write down what they needed to work through their emotional response in the short term, over the summer, and into the following school year. The high degree of relational trust provided an opportunity for teachers to feel comfortable to express their individual emotional needs.

One of the primary reasons we were able to respond to the horrific tragedy that occurred was the healthy emotional/social state of our school community that had been fostered over the years. Our philosophy was deeply anchored in John Dewey's notion of educating the whole child. Equal attention was given to all facets of child development—intellectual, emotional, social, physical, and ethical dimensions of teaching and learning. These factors were evident in the everyday life of the school community.

Each morning and afternoon class began with a class community meeting where children would come together to connect their out-of-school experiences with their school lives. . . . In these 15- to

20-minute class meetings, students felt the power of community and care. Teachers' planning and actions were focused on child-centered curriculum. Thus curriculum was driven by the experiences, interests, and activities that would push critical thinking, and embrace student "voice" and student engagement.

Teachers felt the comfort of knowing that the school and district culture placed a high value on care, responsiveness, openness, connection, and trust.

Teachers experienced strong support for risk taking. New ideas and out-of-the-box thinking was viewed as a critical part of the school culture. As a result, teachers could be entrepreneurial, creative, flexible, and spontaneous.

Teachers supported student risk taking in big and small ways. For several days after the school tragedy, children would often find many print and TV reporters around the school asking questions. Instead of telling the children that they could not speak to the media, we let them know that they had a choice to speak or not. Several teachers had the children role-play how they might be approached and how they may respond. The "teachable" moment became the curriculum throughout the remaining days of the school year and, as often as needed, in the subsequent school years.

In the spring of the year following our school tragedy, several teachers, a psychologist, a social worker, and I were asked to travel to Stockton, California. A school there had experienced a horrific school shooting where more than 30 children had been shot on the playground during lunch recess. Before embarking on the trip, I visited several upper-grade classrooms to ask students for ideas and thoughts that they felt might be valuable to share about what they learned. When asked, "Where do you feel the safest?" I was surprised by the students' almost universal response that the safest place for them was when they were at school, where they were surrounded by caring adults and friends. When asked where they felt the least safe, most would say, "when I'm in my bedroom with the lights out," or often "when I'm playing outside just before it gets dark."

As I reflect on the shooting, I am reminded how the faculty, parents, and staff who were in the building immediately moved to their strengths as a means of responding to the challenges that the tragedy presented. An art teacher sought out a classroom teacher to "partner" in processing the event throughout the day. A parent arrived at school to bring food from a nearby restaurant, a 3rd-grade and 1st-grade teacher decided to bring their children together throughout the day to share their thoughts about the tragedy. The school social worker moved quickly around the building to offer support and direction to parent volunteers who were present when the shooting took place. The important thing was the autonomy that everyone felt, the deep trust, and the way that power and relationships were horizontal.

Instinctually, Teachers Are Eternal Optimists

Lee Keylock

The horrendous murder of elementary students and their teachers in Sandy Hook, Connecticut, in December 2012 is one of the signature horrors of our generation. Here, Lee Keylock, a high school teacher in Sandy Hook, describes beautifully the response of teachers in this community.

"The End and the Beginning," by Wislawa Szymborska (2001)

After every war
someone has to clean up.
Things won't
straighten themselves up, after all.

Someone has to push the rubble
to the sides of the road,
so the corpse-laden wagons
can pass.

Someone has to get mired
in scum and ashes,
sofa springs,
splintered glass,
and bloody rags.

Someone must drag in a girder
to prop up a wall.
Someone must glaze a window,
rehang a door.

Photogenic it's not,
and takes years.
All the cameras have left
for another war.

Again we'll need bridges
and new railway stations.
Sleeves will go ragged
from rolling them up.

Someone, broom in hand,
still recalls how it was.
Someone listens
and nods with unsevered head.
Yet others milling about
already find it dull.

From behind the bush
sometimes someone still unearths
rust-eaten arguments
and carries them to the garbage pile.

Those who knew
what was going on here
must give way to
those who know little.
And less than little.
And finally as little as nothing.

In the grass which has overgrown
causes and effects,
someone must be stretched out,
blade of grass in his mouth,
gazing at the clouds.

I am drawn to Szymborska's poem by instinct. Drawn to it by what Yeats would coin its "terrible beauty." Teachers are compelled by instinct. It's our calling. It's the same song that drives the honeybee to the flower, the young boy to lean in and kiss his first love under a bridge 30 years ago, and the same impulse that drives a baby to grip his mother's hand at birth. The terrible beauty of Szymborska's poem is that it has been almost 2 years since the unfathomable events of December 14. One year and 4 months since the media thrust their cameras unashamedly into our faces to record our expressions bloated with grief. Where are they now? Gone. Left for the next story, the next grim act of motiveless malignancy. And who is left to "rebuild the bridges" for our Beloved Students once they leave the comfort and safety of their grieving parents, the warmth of their homes? It is us. The teachers.

Building is difficult without a blueprint. Ask any contractor. How on Earth were we to help our students, who only days before sat huddled in the corners of their classrooms during the 3-hour lockdown, in the dark, in the awful silence, awaiting the terrible texts? How could we begin to console our colleagues who were in the elementary classrooms of Sandy Hook just 1 mile from the entrance to our own school gates—the ones who barricaded themselves in front of their students—the ones who lost their own lives trying to save the lives of others? How could we erase the sounds of sirens and helicopters that saturated the air outside our classroom windows, forget the personal humiliations of colleagues who had to pee in sinks, or cauterize the image of 1,800 stunned students and teachers who left school that day in complete silence to the onslaught of news crews now lining our streets to record the images of students hand-in-hand as they boarded the buses or fell into the arms of their parents? How in God's name were we to help ourselves?

Instinctually, teachers are eternal optimists. Why else would we spend every waking hour forging lessons to excite and challenge our kids so that learning may occur? Why else would we carry home for the weekends our tote bags laden with papers to grade or tests to correct? We do it because we are eternal romantics—the "hopers" of this world. The great Helen Keller said, "No pessimist ever discovered the secret of the stars, or sailed to an uncharted land, or opened a new doorway for the human spirit." Slam poet Shayne Koyczan asserts, "If your heart is broken, make art with the pieces." So it's what we do. It's what we did. We subscribed to optimism. To love. To beauty. And we did it all without a script. If what we did for our students *felt right*, we did it.

When students returned to school, a few days after the unbearable event, teachers instinctually lined the hallways and lobby to welcome them in an act of true communion. We walked to the gymnasium for a brief assembly and we held hands—all 1,800 of us. We cried. And we were there for one another without uttering any words. The bells to signal classes were canceled. Students were allowed to wander the school freely, visiting those teachers and counselors they felt special bonds with. To have no scheduled classes for the first 2 weeks? No attendance taking? No accountability of where students were or what they were up to? Who could have scripted this administrator's nightmare? But we did it. There was no script for the beauty that happened within our school (and town) over the next few weeks, just instinct and optimism. Students painted in classrooms. Students sat in classrooms listening to their favorite tunes. Some brought their instruments while others sang. And some students wanted to work, wanted to stay mired in worksheets in an attempt to resume some semblance of normality or structure that could distract them from the pain.

Teachers, too, needed help. Counselors were told (and told us) to "just show up." That there is no manual for how to proceed—no training. So we did. One counselor used the analogy of being on an airplane when the oxygen drops; that teachers need to put their masks on first, otherwise they will be of no use to other individuals (our students). Some of the first drops of oxygen were the comfort dogs sent to our school. Images of students hugging these dogs for hours still make me smile. Other images I choose to remember are the young kids who served us breakfast one morning arranged by the Parent Teacher Student Association (PTSA). It was difficult to see the little ones given our new history, but it was also a powerful reminder of why we teach in the first place—the testament to the human spirit and the little torchbearers who will pay it forward. I choose to recollect images of high school students setting up impromptu sports camps and art centers in the buildings of our colonial New England town where for hours they sat with the elementary students and entertained them. These images are the *only* ones that can balance the dreadful ones: the crowds outside the churches, the funerals, the TV crews, and the now-iconic portrait of Lanza's face.

So many acts of generosity filled the school that to list them all would be superfluous. But all the acts of love that were to follow in the next few weeks were our only defiance in the face of the anger and hate that could have ensued (and yes, there were many of those moments, too). We were told to talk. Talk to one another. Talk to the multitude of counselors set up throughout our school. That maybe through narrative we could exorcise our hurt, perhaps illustrate, embrace, and evoke our little joys. Intuitively, I reached out to author Colum McCann and I include the letter to which he graciously responded (and later visited our school). I include the letter to confirm how teachers can answer, do answer, and will always answer to tragedy in order to offer some solace to the ones they care most about—their students.

Dear Mr. McCann,

I am writing to you with heavy heart and the "human instinct for recovery and joy." I am an English teacher at Newtown High School, Sandy Hook, CT, who like so many others is currently dealing with ways to inspire our students in the wake of such trauma. Bottom line, I need your help. We need your help. Perhaps more than help we need your vision.

As English teachers we teach numerous texts and numerous amounts of "tragedy" (is it any wonder we so often commit readicide amongst our youth). While these books have worked in the past, given our unique circumstances this month, they may not work at all. In the aftermath of Sandy Hook I, with a fellow teacher, have been desperately trying to find a text that can "walk the tightrope" between what is real and tragic, yet offer a great sense of hope in the wake of it all. Nothing in our curriculum really speaks to this. Your brilliant novel, *Let the Great World Spin*, could be our answer as it offers such beauty and solace during an unprecedented situation.

I guess what I'm asking for is donation of your book to aid our recovery; a book that I know would engage our youth due to its literary quality, beautifully drawn characters, compelling plot anchored in honest human dilemmas, and, of course, aside from its pure enjoyability, its offering of hope.

I feel a tad awkward asking for such a request (it feels sort of wrong to capitalize on our recent horror), but I have only the students' interests at heart and maybe your book is partly the answer to make, as Ha Jin says, "things beautiful [again], even hailstones in the strawberry fields."

Sincerely,
Lee Keylock

I had no idea what would occur, nor what we even needed. I was just one of *many* teachers trying to seek a little solace for our students, for ourselves. A dreadful script had been written for our school and town (and the world), but this did not mean that a new script could not be written by us. We didn't have to subscribe to the tragic script beyond our control. It was time to rewrite.

Colum came to Newtown High School, and enthusiastically discussed with students the power of narrative and how it promotes empathy through the exchange of stories. His optimism was contagious and mirrored many peoples' desire to help in our time of need. He introduced me to an organization he chairs called Narrative 4, which encourages people to walk in one another's shoes and prove that not only does every story matter, but every life matters. In turn, I and my exceptional teaching colleagues Michelle Toby and Joanna Diaz initiated a story exchange through Narrative 4 that encouraged students to tell essential stories about their lives that were then retold by their peers in their partner's persona. It was cathartic. We were moved by Colum's generosity. It was what we needed. What the students needed. Colum's visit reminded us that we cannot control what the media choose to blitz us with—the images of traumatized teachers and students evacuating Sandy Hook Elementary, the portraits of devastated parents awaiting the dreadful news, the shameful conspiracy theorists who spewed their hate, and the gun control advocates who chose to use the shooting as their platform for debate—but we can impede the flow of that blitz by choosing what we let into our lives, our homes, our TVs, our computers, our cellphones, and so on. Colum's was a *good* memory that gets to replace one of the many strained memories associated with the aftermath of that time.

Thankfully, Newtown is an anomaly. We have been added to that exclusive and chilling list of mass school shootings—a list that leaves us scavenging in the dark looking for some hint of candlelight. In the immediate aftermath of Sandy Hook, our grief was insurmountable—the loss unendurable. Still now I cry as I write. As educators we were asked to help our high school students in any way we could—students who babysat the young victims, tutored them, dated their older brothers or sisters, sat on their front stoops and watched as these children learned to ride their bikes or draw on the sidewalks in chalk. How in God's name could we help, given the varying degrees of grief experienced by our student body, not to mention the varying levels of suffering we, too, as teachers, were enduring? Yet by instinct teachers were, as Szymborska writes, "rolling up their sleeves" and "pushing the rubble to the sides of the roads" that were littered with all the memorials landscaping our town. By instinct we placed "blades of grass in our mouths" in order to "gaze at the clouds" in some instinctual act of empathy and hope—some involuntary act of resilience and love that maybe, just maybe could provide some healing for our students, for our community—perhaps even for the world who sat stunned as they watched.

So as instinctively as I began this piece, so I will end it.

I started with a poem and I will end with a poem (of sorts)—perhaps, to me, one of the greatest poetic references in a work of literature. In the moving scene between Holden Caulfield and the young Phoebe in Salinger's canonic *The Catcher in the Rye*, readers are presented with Holden's idyllic dream born from the Robert Burns poem "Comin' Thro the Rye:"

"I keep picturing all these little kids playing some game in this big field of rye and all. Thousands of little kids, and nobody's around—nobody big, I mean—except me. And I'm standing on the edge of some crazy cliff. What I have to do, I have to catch everybody if they start to go over the cliff—I mean if they're running and they don't look where they're going I have to come out from somewhere and catch them. That's all I'd do all day. I'd just be the catcher in the rye and all. I know it's crazy, but that's the only thing I'd really like to be. I know it's crazy."

I've taught this novel for years and have always been moved to the core by Holden's vulnerability and candidness at this moment (though never until now has it ever rung so true). Our exclusive family—the teachers, the parents, the guidance counselors, the administrators, the community leaders, the students, and so forth—we are all Holdens by nature. We are Holdens simply by default. After all, don't we all believe, instinctually, that however fundamentally far-reaching and altruistic it seems, we can ultimately save our kids—our students—or at least prepare them for the terrible beauty of our world? It's certainly pretty to think so.

8. Mortality in Its Many Forms

When Gabe came to us from middle school, he had already been in and out of battles with leukemia since he was 8. It's a disease that randomly chooses young people and engulfs them, sometimes receding and then rushing back. Sometimes it is actually defeated. But Gabe was not well. He had a fierce circle of friends, some beautiful parents, and a sweet younger brother. He would be in class for a few weeks, then out for treatment.

I never felt so acutely the need to make the readings and class-room discussions compelling, meaningful. This was not about get-ting good test scores or planning a college career. Gabe was getting his chance to "do high school" and he was choosing to spend these months in my classroom. We laughed, we wrote, we did artwork. His skin had a yellowish pallor. He had joined our small school within Berkeley High to be near his friends, Gabriela and Susie, Chloe and Matt, and others. And because we would pay attention to him, see him as a whole person.

When 10th grade started, I had students fill out a questionnaire. Under goals, Gabe wrote, "Graduate from high school." Mainly, he said he just wanted to be "normal." But many days, he was not able to be in school. The bone graft had not worked and he was fading. His friends gathered at lunch and after school, shared who would visit and when. The days ticked by. Finally one Wednesday it happened. Gabriela stuck her head in my classroom with that "look" and I knew that she had gotten paged, the news had come that Gabe had died. I went out with her and we had permission from the principal to go to other classes, collect the friends. They flowed and stumbled and ran to the classroom, weeping and hugging. Soon a delegation split off to go right to his house, to hug and cry with his parents.

Although I am primarily addressing student deaths from the epidemic of violence in our society, teachers find themselves at the pivot point at other fatal moments. And many of the same challenges confront the classroom here: the sense of loss, of helplessness, of fear and awe. The same questions of guilt or responsibility, as far-fetched as that may seem. It is still the teacher who must mourn and feel the loss while at the same time helping the class, the community, move forward.

Recently a post went up on a Facebook group I belong to: "So, here is a heartbreaking question for my badass teachers group: Have you ever had experience with the death of a student? Last Monday one of my students, an 8-year-old boy, died in a boating accident. To address my personal sorrow and that of my fellow teachers, are any of you aware of songs, poems, etc., that express what teachers go through when facing such tragedy? On the web there seem to be ample ideas for how teachers can help students but not specific info on how to help the very real and different pain of the teacher. It's almost as if the expectation is that we as professionals should not have difficulty beyond how to help our students. As much as I feel terribly for the family and child's friends, the honest truth is I also feel very sorry for all of us teachers who loved that little soul! We all need comfort." She got hundreds of responses. So many teachers had experience with such terrible moments; so many wanted to share.

More and more stories poured on to the page, such as this: "I'm so sorry. Two years ago one of my students' fathers was murdered in a random act of violence and it was probably one of the most difficult times I've had in my career. I know people who have lost students (cancer, accidents, suicide, murder), but I have been fortunate that it has never happened to me. I think just loving one another is the only way to get through: all of you together, kids, teachers, and the family. Again, I am SO sorry for your loss!"

And dozens of ideas appeared, like this: "I did two things to help my students. One is that we went outside and drew chalk drawings of whatever made them happy. We didn't write the student's name or anything but just put happy things for other students to see (hearts, rainbows, funny words, and so on). It got us all laughing and smiling. I also put papers on their desks of a chart of cartoon faces with different emotions. When we had independent writing (I'm an English teacher), they could write about whatever they wanted and had that graphic as a springboard. I didn't force them to write about their lost class-mate, but it was an option."

This is a teacher practice that has no official sanction, not even any acknowledgment, but it is a central aspect of our lives in the classroom.

When a recent spate of suicides at Gunn High School took five lives and saw many more attempts, an anonymous teacher wrote a long, searching piece for the local outlet, *Palo Alto On-line*.[1] Among her observations:

> Venturing now, though, from still-unknown causes of the suicides to the ways in which we—the school district, Gunn and the community—have coped, I can make some observations. . . .
>
> First, the attention at school to the day-to-day weight of grief and loss has been uneven: teachers sometimes encouraged to depart from business as usual, sometimes not; workloads sometimes reduced, sometimes not; teachers coping on their own with situations for which nothing has prepared them: an empty desk suddenly present in the classroom but 20 or 30 students still assembling day after day, as if at a memorial service that cannot end.
>
> Second, our handling of the vexing problem of "drawing too much attention" to the suicides has been equivocal:

1. Available at http://paloaltoonline.com/news/show_story.php?id=18127

students forbidden to congregate at school in sorrow (their chalked tributes, sometimes, hosed away) but permitted to decorate much of the campus with upbeat messages of hope; a leadership policy of "no comment" to the press, but with exceptions.

Third, our stance toward youths' mental troubles has been awkward: a wish to reach out to students with psychological problems but leaving it up to them to come to Adolescent Counseling Services on campus rather than having the counselors visit classrooms; a desire to help troubled students feel safe but without due attention to some students' mockery of those who are absent from school due to personal problems or to some teachers' and coaches' anger at and impatience with the suicides, as well as their discomfort in handling public reactions.

While murders take the lives of about 4,800 youth a year, more than 5,000 teens in the United States die in automobile accidents and 400,000 are injured. About 4,600 teens die of suicide, the vast majority being boys. Some 2,500 people under the age of 21 die of cancer each year. There are so many other ways that the terrible finger of fate points at our students. And for each of these tragedies, there is a classroom; there is a teacher.

> And for each of these tragedies, there is a classroom; there is a teacher.

Losing Kyle—Automobile Accident

Hasmig Minassian

Hasmig Minassian is lead teacher of the Communication Arts and Sciences small school at Berkeley High School.

I live in fear of the communication of bad news, both the giving and the receiving. It seems the worst part is not being able to anticipate your own reaction or that of others. Once we know everything, we can handle it. Once we have all the pieces in front of us, we can arrange them or marvel at their disarray. Four weeks before Kyle and his friend PJ were killed, I watched my own 4-year-old son plummet from the top of a rock at a local park and crack his femur. Riding down the hill in the ambulance, I called his other mom to share the bad news and implement an action plan. Painful as it was, there was something to do that could fix the problem, an empowering feeling for a first responder. As a teacher, communicating about my student Kyle's death and its immediate aftermath was the first challenge. Death feels like a dead end. Where do we go from dead? He and PJ died on a Wednesday afternoon over spring break. Luckily I was in town, but many students and teachers were not. When my student Leib called, the news felt like a hot potato. I felt a tremendous burden being the only adult at the school in the know. Who do I tell first? Adults? Kids? In the moment, I chose to send out a mass text to my colleagues and a mass Facebook message to our students in the Communication Arts and Sciences (CAS) small school within Berkeley High School. I was scared, unclear how to proceed.

3/31/10, 10:30 P.M.
Horrible, awful news and no other way to tell you

My dear CAS Juniors, I hate to have to do this over Facebook, since it's so impersonal, but I need all of you to know as quickly as possible that Kyle Strang was killed this afternoon in a really tragic car accident off of Richmond Parkway. He was driving with a friend and lost control of the car, hit a school bus, and was killed instantly. I know the shock will be felt for quite some time—and there is nothing more to say but express the tragedy and loss we all feel with Kyle's absence.

As soon as I get any information about services, I'll let you know.

Please support one another and be together as we process this loss. I will be at school on Monday.

Love, Ms. Minassian

Several of Kyle's closest friends came right over. These were kids who had stopped by while my son was convalescing to drop off food or baked goods. They knew where I lived and I was close with some of their parents from previous years in education, so it felt right to say "yes" to their requests. When you teach in a small community, even without a major tragedy, the lines of intimacy with students and their families can be blurry. Kids have your cellphone number. Parents invite you for dinner. You are not quite friends. You are not quite family. But you aren't business associates, either. It's a nebulous relationship that lacks clear rules and structure.

Late that evening, it became abundantly clear that everyone needed a place to gather. The community needed a central location. With school out for 5 more days, I made a quick decision to open our home the following night to anyone who needed a place to be together. In hindsight, this was the single best decision I made for CAS and for Kyle's family but one that would have the most severe consequences for my long-term emotional well-being.

4/1/10, 9:04 A.M.

I am opening our house up tonight, 5:30–9, for CAS kids who wants/needs a place to be. I'm at _____ address. We should know more by then about services, etc. xo Minassian

Teachers are quick thinkers. This is our charge as we manage a classroom full of dynamic energy and vibrant intellect. We can't always know what the ripple effects of our action will be, so we make the best decision we can in a moment. That night at my house was extraordinary. Not only did dozens of adults and kids come together in grief and community, but Kyle's father, Craig, and stepmother, Persis, also joined us. When they walked in, I felt suddenly unprepared. It's one thing to manage your own grief and the grief of your students, but to be in the presence of a man who just lost his son, barely 24 hours before, is almost unbearable. By opening my own home to students in grief, and now parents in grief, I crossed a personal/professional boundary that would take years to recover. Had the timing been different, all of this gathering and grieving would have been done in the context we all know: school. But the invitation to my home changed the optics of Kyle's death. Suddenly it belonged to me 24 hours a day, and I belonged to it. Again, I composed a reflection on Facebook that night for the community.

4/2/10, 12:18 A.M.
Candlelight Vigil and Service Information for Kyle

Hi All,

Great to see so many of you today and really felt the love in the room for Kyle and the support you truly have for one another. As many of you have already said, we will pull through this one day and one step at a time, and only all together.

Here are some important events to honor Kyle going on this weekend.

FRIDAY 4/2: A Candlelight Vigil near his mom's house, _____, 7:30 P.M.; wear bright colors and bring a candle if you have one.

SUNDAY 4/4, Funeral Services for Kyle will start at 1:00 P.M. at Temple Emanu-el at _____.

After the funeral, there will be a burial at a gravesite (optional) about 20 minutes away, and after that, a gathering at Kyle's dad's house at _____ where Prentice's family will also be available, as they live across the street.

There will be an altar at the funeral so bring anything you can leave as a symbol of Kyle.

On Monday we will come up with a plan in CAS classes for how to cope, process, and move forward. We'll support the family in the ways we know how and continue to be there for one another. Love to you all, Ms. Minassian

Perhaps the most poignant symbol of my professional world eclipsing my personal one is the decision I made to return to work the following Monday. I was on week 4 of a 6-week leave to care for my son who was immobilized in a body cast and a wheelchair. My students needed me more than my son in that moment, so I sent him back to his preschool (which graciously took him in) so I could roll up my sleeves and care for my other kids. In truth, this worked out well for my son. He was ready to be around other 4-year-olds and enjoy a more stimulating educational environment. His school created a curriculum around accommodating for people's physical disabilities and he reconnected with his own beloved teachers and classmates. But once again it sent a message to my own school community that I was flexible, available, and willing to make personal sacrifices to keep the pieces together. If they *needed* me more, than I needed to *give* them more, right? It's a hard lesson we learn as teachers, even under normal circumstances. Students and families will make their needs clear but we can't, won't, and shouldn't always try to meet them.

So Monday morning April 5 arrived and I returned to work, my son returned to school, and our work as a community began. Below is a communication to families about that day:

Dear CAS Junior Families,

At Kyle's memorial services yesterday, the officiator, Magid Jhos Singer, depicted the aftermath of Kyle's death as us "slogging on," heavy-hearted and slowly, intentionally, piecing our lives together as we imagine this next stage without him. He encouraged us to simultaneously sit with the pain of Kyle's loss and embrace that the work ahead of us was going to be challenging and uphill, but very necessary work indeed. With those words in mind, I returned home last night thinking about our dear CAS Juniors and how on Earth we would face them this morning. I am writing to update you on where we are as a staff, as a class, and as a community as we cope with the void that Kyle's death has left us.

This morning the CAS staff met to discuss how we might approach our students in their grief, support each of them where they were, and acknowledge the wide range of impact this has had on them. Each grade level agreed to address it and give students a chance to write, speak, or both. The CAS Juniors started their day with me. The first thing we did in class was to write to the prompt: "What scared you most about coming to school today? What thoughts/feelings/anxieties do you have being here today?" Students wrote for 20 minutes and shared out sporadically. I have excerpted the range of responses below.

"I was a little scared to come today because I knew it would be a way depressing and sad moment. I was also anxious to come because I saw so many of the CAS Juniors this weekend and we feel comfortable being around each other."

"I still expect to see him today. I can't accept the fact that he is gone."

"No one I know this well has died before so I don't know how to deal with this. It still feels so unreal."

"I lost two good friends in the same day and I'm just stuck. I don't know what to do."

"We need each other more than anything right now and I am afraid school might take that away. Everyone's thoughts are spinning, making regular work much more difficult."

"I fear it will take me a very long time before I start to feel okay. I fear seeing my friends who are okay because we are in such different places. I am scared that things will move too fast for me in school."

"Life will move again, but not now. Right now it is on pause. I am still and quiet inside."

"We are back at school with our school family but someone is missing. I fear that people will start to cry and won't be able to get through the day."

"I don't like to see people cry or be sad."

"My anxiety is when Kyle's death DOES sink in, what will it be like? What will it be like when I realize what this death means?"

"I'm scared to be in a car with my friends, especially on a rainy day. I had a nightmare about that last night. I don't want to drive fast."

"When I was at your house, it didn't feel real. But now, I came into class today, and I know he's actually gone. He shouldn't have left like that. He had so much to live for."

"I feel like CAS is never going to be the same. I also now fear that one of my family members might die because Kyle was like family."

"My big fear is never seeing Kyle again and that school won't ever be the same."

"My fear is that one day we're really just going to forget everything and I don't want that to happen."

"I believe that we as a community will overcome this. Supporting his family is also a part of this so we can all overcome it together."

"My thoughts are confused, anguished, and devastated. Who knows when I'll catch up?"

"The whole thing has torn me to pieces and made me so scared. Now life is getting real. I know Kyle had plans. Why did he have to go? I didn't even have plans. I'm so unmotivated and so lost. I miss him."

"A large fear of mine today is not showing enough grief or sadness. I've always been reserved when showing myself to others. I'm worried about people judging me. One of my biggest fears is that Kyle will fade out of our minds. "

"It is really hard to walk into class and not see Kyle. I can't accept that he's gone."

"I'm really just in shock that this could happen and life can be so short."

"Today I feel like I have nothing to say."

"My heart is heavy. I fear that I will never get over this. Every day will be a new challenge"

"I don't want to keep being reminded and then be even more sad than I already am."

"It hurts me to see people cry about this. I understand. I just don't think it's hit me yet."

"I don't know what I am feeling today. I have a knot in my stomach. I keep thinking about how easily it could have been anyone else. If someone had told me this would happen, I wouldn't believe it."

"I know that without his everyday presence, we'll be able to keep his spirit alive because of how strong and tight knit we are. Every hair stands on my body and my breath deepens when I think about all that has happened."

I also shared with them some writing I did in response to this prompt. Here is an excerpt from that:

"But I worry if we stop talking about him or hugging about him or processing his death, that he'll slip away somehow unnoticed. Every time we are talking about the Great Depression or civil rights, we're not talking about Kyle and I fear he will disappear from us. I ask myself, how do we keep Kyle's spirit in the room but give ourselves the permission to move on without his body? It really is permission that we're asking for—the permission to move forward—to think about your futures for a moment, to smile about my son getting his cast off in a week, to look forward to our overnight in Santa Cruz, your civil rights research paper, and to send you off into the summer before your senior year with pride, all while keeping Kyle with us."

So you see we have quite a task ahead of us. Many of the kids came up to me after class and said just writing these thoughts down helped release them of the burden of carrying them around. The rest of the class period was spent discussing plans for remembering Kyle. These include retiring his desk in two classes, planning a student memorial for him (date TBA), organizing his yearbook memorial page, and other ideas kids have for commemorating who Kyle was. Further into the day, they were able to continue processing with their CAS teachers, talking about ideas for a memorial video in Ms. Rasiah's class, and a book of some kind of the kids' writing for Kyle's families in Ms. Martinez's class. They also had a chance to share in Mr. Boltz's class. Students were also offered a space to go if they needed to be out of any of their classes for any reason. Ms. Offermann and a counselor from the Health Center are available all week and next in room C338 for kids who need it.

As for class this week and next and my schedule: We are starting a new project, the 20s and 30s metaphor one, and I do expect the kids to start producing some work. It will be a long haul, I know—and slow sometimes, but I think beginning a routine for them with academics will be important for the healing process.

As long as we keep Kyle with us in the ways we've set up, I think kids will respond positively. And all the sadness and grief? Well, I think we need to keep honoring it, keep allowing the space for it, and keep hugging them through this. I know most of your teens are not big talkers when it comes to their parents, and I feel blessed that they've been so open in sharing with me and the rest of the CAS staff, but this recovery will certainly be a community effort, so I just ask that if you see something that concerns you at home, you let me know—and we will do the same on our end. We are keeping a very close eye on the kids for the next little while and will alert you to any signs we see that might require more than our hugs, love, and support.

Thanks for getting all the way through this email. I thought it was critical that you knew what was going on in class and that we kept in close contact as we struggle to help our kids, and ourselves deal with this tragedy. Kyle's dad, Craig, spoke eloquently at the funeral about how their greatest gift was hearing the stories that Kyle's CAS friends/family had to share about their son. We have always known this community was special but in this past week it has been truly magical and Kyle, along with your kids, can take most of the credit for that. Each of them is a blessing to me.

Please contact me or other CAS staff if you have any questions or concerns,

Warmly,

Hasmig Minassian

Sarah Crews, a close friend of Kyle's father Craig, wrote a song honoring Kyle titled "I Need a Boat". In it, she sings, "A thousand hearts were broken but ten thousand more were opened when your soul dropped to the ocean sending waves out to the shore." Kyle's death has given me gifts I don't yet fully understand, including lifelong friendships with his family, deep relationships with the young adults who are his friends, and the calculus on my capacity as a human being. And it has changed me forever as a teacher. Kyle brought out the best in his loved ones through his own passion for life and his dedication to a cause. He ignited a fire in me to be a better teacher, to push his writing and his often politically irrational beliefs. His death taught me that my role as teacher, however critical, is limited. And we can't know those limits until they are tested. But I have no regrets. I did what I knew best to do at that time. As a teacher, when you are responsible for the perfect execution of each singular moment in your classroom, all you can do is trust your intuition, leap, and give thanks for the chance to reflect, learn, and grow.

It's hard to look back and say that I'd change a thing about my role as Kyle's teacher in the aftermath of his death. It's analogous to regretting the marriage and subsequent divorce that resulted in your child. You can't really say "If I had to do it again . . ." because it would change the entire course of your life. Life doesn't work that way. You can't tease it apart and only keep the blessings. If I had to do it again? Kyle and PJ wouldn't have died. Period. Everything after that was just physics.

Remembering Angél

Godhuli Bose

Godhuli Bose is an English teacher at El Cerrito High School in California.

November 12, 2013—Facebook post

Early this morning, a very beloved student of mine, Angél Gutierrez, 16 years old, decided to take his life, by jumping in front of a BART train at El Cerrito Del Norte station. He's been with me for 3 beautiful years and I watched him grow up in front of me. He was tall, handsome, with a lovely nut brown complexion and a naughty grin that lit up the room when he smiled. He was also partially deaf. He was such a brave, gentle, funny young man and I always complimented him when he frequently showed up in class wearing bright red lipstick, a girlfriend's shirt or jacket, black nail polish. Once I brought over a bag of jewelry I was going to give away. Angél spent a long time going through the bag and decorated himself with necklaces, earrings, and bracelets he found. He looked more gorgeous than I could ever look in my jewelry. He carried himself so well I told him he could be the next, most famous celebrity crossdresser/ supermodel and that as soon as he graduated I would be his manager.

I told him we could both make a lot of money with this plan. He giggled like a happy baby and promised me that he would model for our World Language event in spring. His last essay earned him a solid A in my class, his first A ever in English. He had metaphors, similes, dialogue, and a strong plot and conflict all in three pages. I put the essay on the document camera and we read his essay in class together. But we are not always able to appreciate the angels God sends us. And I am sure he had to hear many negative, cruel remarks in school for being different. No wonder he felt such extreme loneliness, such sadness. We all need a place in this world. It is our inability as a society to cherish someone who was headstrong and smart enough to be different from other boys, who was funny enough to have so many friends, interpreters, and teachers who loved him, but he still fell through the cracks and willfully jumped in front of a moving train this morning. Angél was teaching us a lesson. Be kind, be kind, be kind. Don't hate what you don't understand.

Sometimes, when one lives in too much solitude, as Angél did, because of his condition, the burden gets too heavy and we crack under the strain. After all, only a demigod like Atlas could carry the world on his shoulders. Not a good idea for us lesser mortals. Suicide and the desire to give up on life is not a permanent desire. It is fleeting gossamer. It comes and goes. But when that feeling arrives at your doorstep, knocking loudly to be let in, and it is a stormy night, we collapse and get sucked into that miasma, and it feels like a permanent nightmare. It is only good friends, a loving family, a strong passion for something we practice, and love that sees us through those dark stormy nights. And suicidal people always know that night may come again, quite like cutters, though that is a different conversation.

This afternoon after he transitioned, I saw that last night he had sent me a friend request on Facebook. I friended him today, even though he has left us, and I hope he is smiling up there, looking down at us fondly, with forgiveness. Last Friday he came to class wearing blue nail polish and some eye makeup. I made everyone in class cheer for him saying, "Here is a student who is a REAL man.

Look! He has the courage to be who he wants to be." He took a piece of paper and pressed his lips on it, leaving his lipstick stain, and wrote, "A kiss for you" I tacked it on the wall. It is still there. Little did I know, that was his last good-bye card to me. I miss you, son. I wish I had held you in my arms longer and stronger. I miss you. I miss you.

9. Teacher Education

This book does not suggest that there are easy solutions or even explanations. And certainly those in the counseling department have done more direct consideration of grieving and loss, how to talk about it. But there is a big hole in teacher education when we never consider, don't address, cannot imagine what to do when students die. When I mention to people that I am thinking of writing some thoughts on what to do when students die, sadly, everyone I know who is teaching in cities remarks immediately:

- Yes! We need that!
- I experienced that.
- I was at a total loss.

Being the teacher at the front of a class that has lost a student is a nightmare we each experience but seldom share. It is time we opened up this discussion in teacher education, in staff development, in school spaces.

When I was new to teaching, I learned so much, and engaged so many students, using Luis Rodríguez's memoir of his own gang life, *Always Running* (2005). I have taken students to meet him and have talked to him whenever I could. And when I discovered his book *Hearts and Hands, Creating Community in Violent Times* (2001), I knew he was someone who finally understood, who could actually bring some wisdom to the question, and who could suggest the link between our project of creating classroom community and the lived lives of these young people. Here are some things Rodríguez made me think of while I was reflecting on his book.

Sadly, we usually think of education as a matter of creating the individual unit, the rational economic actor striving for his or her own competitive success. But the reality is that humans live in a world of interlocking relationships, even dependency. Childhood to adulthood is not a journey of individuation; it is introduction into community. Moreover, we exist in a complex ecology of humans and other life-forms. Looking at virtually every society until the last hundred years, we see that young people need to exist in an extended world of responsible adults. They need to learn the ways and customs of various overlapping communities. And they need to be kids before they are required to be adults.

> Childhood to adulthood is not a journey of individuation; it is introduction into community.

Rodríguez cites Michael Meade's observation that the work of community elders is "holding the ground while youth make their glorious mistakes." Too often, the only thing that brings youth and elders together is trouble. When society fails to develop true eldership and mentoring at the most basic community level, and when elders are not there to provide compassion, wisdom, experience, and meaningful and lasting knowledge, the young usually "sacrifice" themselves to drugs, violence, gangs, and prisons, many times paying with their own lives.

In constructing the schools that we need, that our students need, we are responsible to make communities that matter to the youth. This is not about "rescuing" young people. We can't rescue them because they have to save themselves, tapping into their own creative energies. But our communities can be intentional, can challenge young people to engage their world with critical clarity while providing adult support as they mature. They have to become masters of their own lives—with their autonomy and integrity strengthened in the process.

In seeking to build communities that can transform lives, Rodríguez (2001) suggests that we must ask ourselves the following questions:

- Where are the centers and schools where young people can be creative, respected, and safe?
- Where are the meaningful social activities, including community-organized and community-sanctioned recreation, as well as the empowering, socially charged, community improvement projects?
- Where are the loving family environments? Where these environments don't exist, is it fair—or wise—to blame the families?
- Where are the sanctuaries, the safe and sacred spaces, where their spiritual quests are attended to, their psychological and social concerns are met, and where the law, which often works against them, can be accessible and understandable so it can work for them?
- Do the young have the sense that their floundering steps, even the missteps, are part of their growth and advancement?
- How can youths contribute to social change, to bettering their homes and community, to know that their contributions are essential? (p. 51)

Rodríguez (2001) concludes, "Other societies have long recognized that young people need proper initiatory experiences, rites of passage profound enough to match the fire in their souls. If not, they will turn that fire outward, burning everything around them, acting out in violent ways, or consuming themselves in such false initiations as drugs and alcohol" (p. 51).

It is wrong, criminally wrong, to consign community building in the classroom to some granola, feel-good activity that is subordinate to the "rigor" (or rigor mortis) of the academic content. It is not just "social emotional context" here and the important stuff there. For there is no learning, there is no thinking, without community. Some schools are not set up to support the building of community, within the class or across the classrooms. If that is the case, the task of teachers with a commitment to social justice is to fight for community, to change the context and conditions. And to the extent that the bureaucracy won't allow that, then our task is to identify the limitations imposed by the structures, expose these limitations, to help the students make the criticism, so that their suffering will not happen in silence.

Addressing the Issue in the Academy

Leora Wolf-Prusan

Leora Wolf-Prusan is a former teacher who recently received her EdD from UCLA. Here she describes her work to include the issue of student death and how schools respond into the discourse of schooling.

At the time, I wasn't a classroom teacher anymore; I had joined an education nonprofit that partnered with high schools around the Bay Area. It was, at times, meaningful work. In my role I was an insider-outsider: I worked with teachers and mainly their senior classes, built relationships and connections, but wasn't part of the fabric of the school.

When Ditiyan was killed, I found out through another student calling me. I was sitting in my parents' living room in San Francisco. It was a double hit: first the death of Ditiyan shot biking home from school 2 weeks before graduation, and second, containing the space for this young man's grief who was taking care of me while talking on the phone. "I just thought you should know," he said softly, and we made arrangements for me to pick him and his friends up the following week at school and we'd go to the funeral together.

This was May 2011, and I already had been accepted to an EdD program and decided to move down to Los Angeles to get my doctorate in education that fall.

Entering the program, I knew that educator wellness would be my focus. Having worked in multiple high schools, I had accumulated years of watching and hearing teachers care for others without being cared for themselves. Their own trauma and processing of chronic stress and violence had (and has) left them disenfranchised. As the program ensued, it became clear that my focus would narrow and I would research how urban high school teachers experienced the homicides of their students.

But first I had to prove to the Ivory Tower that this was a real problem. Professors repeatedly questioned if this was a large enough sociological/political/psychological/pedagogical problem to study. How would I "prove" that the death of a student translated to a change in teaching and learning? Was this my own grief speaking? "Oh, so intense" was a frequent reaction. Yes, it is. But it is also so human. How could the field of "urban" education not be talking about student homicide and how we teachers experience it?

I created an informal survey to prove to my program this was a problem worth examining. Via social media, I cast a fairly small net: "Have you ever experienced student death?" How much? When? Where? What was that like?

In less than 48 hours, the responses were overwhelming: More than 34 educators from across the country responded, most of whom I did not know. They wrote long, passionate passages about how the death(s) of their students profoundly impacted them both personally and professionally.

Then there was the challenge of proposing to study the chronic, gang, and gun-related violent deaths of students. Not episodic, not suburban-based onetime shooting events but ongoing, compounded violence that is hard to fix, hard to identify the root of the pain, and predominately lives in disenfranchised and stigmatized communities that do not garner a national sense of urgency. Chronic and compounded violence is the type of trauma that Howard, Feigelman, Li, et al. (2002) describes as "non-war time exposure to violence by urban children," a violence that has "occurred with such unparalleled frequency that the neighborhoods in which they reside have become known as 'war zones' of a different kind" (p. 456). Yes, Newtown was and is important, but so too are the corners in Deep East Oakland Bay Area, blocks of Venice, California, and the streets of Chicago.

I brought this as "proof" to my university and off I went. At my preliminary oral defense, I began with Ditiyan's story, and then a slide with each face of every Oakland homicide victim's face under the age of 24 in the year 2012; they comprised 33 of the 131 homicides (25% of total homicides) that year. My point? This phenomenon is real and it is human. Each one of those faces has known and potentially impacted multiple teachers, multiple educators.

With my committee's blessing, I launched my study. Or so I thought. The school district that has the highest rate of youth homicide in an urban region denied my request for research, stating that they could not find significance or relation to their strategic plan (this, of course, was even after the principals and teachers of said district agreed enthusiastically to my study). When I did find a local district that approved my study, the challenge was to find principals who would allow me to speak to teachers at the site. "We don't deal with community violence here," one wrote. "You should be looking at the White suburbs." A common response was that "we only want to focus on positive issues here on campus; your study might exacerbate stigma we are trying to erase." All of these are valid concerns.

My concern was that—yet again—district and administration were blocking teachers' opportunity to develop their own coherent narrative around their experience. It echoes classic secondary trauma theory: Institutions that are supposed to support us often exacerbate trauma instead.

Then back to the academic challenge: Was this a psychological study? Anthropological? Sociological? I was tasked with making this project quantitative enough to give the subject merit and validation yet qualitative enough to give the subject heart and integrity. In the end, I collected 146 surveys from teachers across the district and interviewed 16 teachers in depth. The phenomenon was and is real. As it turns out, it is more than just "my issue."

Along this journey I've joked that I should have started a blog capturing people's reactions when I tell them what I am studying. Anyone who has worked in our public schools in chronically stressed communities will usually either (1) begin to cry or (2) unload stories upon stories of students who have died. I kept thinking, we are keeping these big, real feelings and events locked up inside of us, waiting for a trigger. How can we respond to what teachers need after the death of their students if we do not take the time (1) for teachers themselves to reflect on the experience and (2) to ask teachers what they need?

When I traveled to high schools throughout the district that finally approved my study and presented the opportunity to participate, teachers pulled me over after my presentations to share their experiences. Those who get it, get it.

The findings are striking.

I looked into how student violent deaths impact teachers as teaching professionals, and examined what factors influenced their meaning-making and resilience-building after the gang/gun-related death. Most important for me, I studied what supports teachers need after their students are killed.

First, experiencing a student violent death caused teachers to become more empathetic and caring toward their students; the socioemotional aspect of teaching became more important to teachers. After going to one of his students' memorial service, one teacher told me that his student's death "really lets me see under the surface as students. There are people that care about them; there are people that love them. They've had a background." After a student is killed, teachers' relationships with current students become more conscientious, empathetic, and socioemotionally centered.

Moreover, experiencing a student homicide caused teachers to assume new protection and intervention roles professionally. In my research, all but one teacher (15 out of 16, or 94%) noted the direct connection between experiencing a student violent death and the resulting need to protect current students from situations that they perceive as endangering. One teacher reflected on his new role of teacher as protector: "Honestly, I felt like, fuck, we gotta protect them. . . . So does it impact it? Yes. What does it makes us do? It makes us protect them more. It makes [our principal] go down the hall every Tuesday and Thursday, after school; obviously he doesn't get paid for it, but he opens the gym, you know why? So they're not

out there. We do after-school clubs, why? So they're not out there.
... We want to protect them."

Second, student violent deaths create a sense of threat fear for
teachers' own personal safety. Multiple teachers described being
in public places and planning out escape routes. Despite the fact
that their students were killed off campus in the community, the
suddenness of gang-related gun violence resulted in expressions of
high anxiety and fear.

Third, the practice of honoring the killed student is a crucial fac-
tor in teachers' building resilience after the death of their student.
Schools can influence teachers' resiliency by allowing individuals
in a community to rise to their own resilience by naming and addressing the death event. Plaques, memorial services, ribbons, and
murals are not trivial: They are important markers for teachers' own
processing and meaning-making regarding the event.

Fourth, teachers need to connect with colleagues who share
student death experience for support. Across all five regions I studied, eight participants explicitly named the need to connect with
colleagues who taught or had a relationship with the killed student as essential to the supports they need. Teachers reported feeling alone and not having anyone to turn to, or said that they did
not want the services provided by the district through the school.
Teachers called for teacher-led support groups, not district-provid-
ed services, both for short-term and long-term support.

Lastly, how school systems communicate and disseminate information about the student death and the death aftermath (i.e., the
memorial) informs if and how teachers experience support. Teachers want and need information about the death event and death
aftermath (i.e., the memorial or funeral), and importantly, they want
to be told in person. Teachers recounted hearing about a student
shot over the intercom while they taught, or seeing their student's
name on the news, or reading about it on a flyer put in their box
before they began their teaching day. Teachers need validation and
affirmation to help them cope, to have all the information available
to try to make sense of something so senseless.

At the end of each interview, I asked teachers what the interview experience itself had been like for them. Some remarked that they didn't realize they were carrying so much pain about the student's death. Two male teachers cried throughout the interview, and reflected that they don't allow themselves to think about their own grief experience.

There are two quotes from separate interviews that keep echoing in my head:

"Anyone who says this isn't worth talking about is disconnected. You don't have to come from it to be touched by it. . . . Your study is viable. I'm not the only one with multiple deaths. Especially being in this neighborhood, or choosing to teach in this neighborhood, you're signing on for that. It's part of the package. Do you choose to be a part of it? It's going to happen. I anticipate it. Do I look at a kid and say, 'Oh, are you going to be one of them?' I hope not. But you just don't know."

And,

"In some ways [this interview] almost feels empowering to me. It's like acknowledging that I have made it through something like this. I'm not trying to take anything away from the kids. I feel like I'm kind of a survivor of this, too. And if it does happen again—and I hope it doesn't—I do have coping skills, but I really had to fish them out for myself. It's made me feel better and has given a voice to what I've gone through and has acknowledges that this is not an easy thing to go through, not something to sweep under the rug. Teachers too experience it."

My study voices the need for teachers' experience of their students' violent deaths to be recognized, honored, and supported. I've been honored to hear and capture teachers' narratives. Their resilience has been a part of my own continued healing.

School systems must address that they have the power to either support their employees or perpetuate teachers' trauma by disenfranchising their experiences. If student gang/gun-related deaths cause teachers to humanize their students, so too can these deaths cause us to professionalize our teachers who are the unacknowledged first responders and gatekeepers of healing.

After Meleia died there was an uncomfortable division. Not a split, really, but certainly a divergence of perspectives. Those who graduated in 2002 were closer to Santana and tried to give him some support even as they were horrified and saddened by Meleia's death. Those from 2003 knew Meleia better and were focused on her, looking at Santana as the embodiment of evil.

As I mentioned above, I was amazed that the judge gave Santana 24 years. Yes, the killing was horrible, awful, unforgivable. And if someone had killed Meleia by being a drunk driver it would be the same: horrible and unforgivable. But 24 years? Would he even survive? Was his life over? And most important, I wonder what Meleia would want. Fiercely opposed to the massive prison system, she would, I think, hope for some other resolution, one more in line with restorative justice principles.

When I would visit Santana, I had no intention of going easy on him or even of being his friend. And I certainly did not want to be his hope and lifeline, something all prisoners desperately need. But I wanted to understand, to know more about him and how he ended up here. I wanted to know more about those last hours of Meleia's life, too.

I learned a lot and very little. We talked about everything. He was curious just about the world out here, my life, our lives, and he told plenty of prison stories. And sometimes he said things that struck me dumb.

He described being the outsider, the East Oakland kid, the tough kid who bounced around schools and ended up at Berkeley High, falling in with a group of middle-class students, both Black and White. He got a lot out of these relationships—enjoyed the friendships, gained access to more resources, and had a great time. They got something out of it, too—Santana's great generosity and sense of humor, but also his street cred, his tough rep from being who he was. He was their road dog and they got something out of it. I wondered whether, in this unequal friendship, it was perhaps inevitable that when one night something went terribly wrong, Santana would of course be the one ending up in prison.

He described one moment that has stayed with me ever since: "I remember being at a party in Berkeley, you know, with Jesse and Fritz. Everyone was having a good time but I was sitting on the side. There was one other Black guy there kinda lightweight muggin' me and I was wondering if I was going to get out of there without a fight. I was jumpy. I looked over at Jesse and Fritz and they were dancing, just rocking their heads back, eyes closed, not a care in the world. And I thought to myself, 'I wish. I just wish I could feel that free, that care-free, even for a day.'" That wish, that longing, marks the fissures—both visible and invisible—that run through our society. He was a friend but never quite part of that middle-class world. He was an outsider and lived in a world that was more dangerous.

And it made me think: To be a teacher means to try to understand such fissures, to read more deeply the social terrain of youth. It also means to be always on the side of the youth.

If we fail to address the real world in which these young people are living, we fail them. For you certainly cannot advance academic outcomes when your student is dead, or your students are in constant fear of losing a classmate. We teachers find ourselves trying desperately to keep the class together, to stop this one from cutting, stop that one from dropping out, and stop the other from dying. In time, we learn that teaching is a process of holding on and letting go—sometimes in small, routine ways, sometimes on the most transcendent levels. But our classrooms, our students, are in this together. We desperately work to get our students to connect with and care about this space; and we ourselves begin to identify with the students before us.

If we fail to address the real world in which these young people are living, we fail them

So I come back to the same point. Education is not simply about individual success, individual competition. It is about community and the ways we need one another. Only by building such community can we respond to the calamities that life deals us. And only by responding through community can we envision a world of greater solidarity, justice, and joy.

There is a bench right by the tree where Meleia was slain—a long cement bench with a small wall behind it. On another July 17, the second anniversary of her death, a group of friends and friends' parents and teachers descended on the spot and spent a day decorating this small alcove. Each of us was given a square tile and paint to create whatever artistic devotional we wanted—words, images, feelings—for the back wall. The pieces emerged, before being taken to be fired: a butterfly, flowers, "rest in power," a fist, "love," a sunrise. Some had brought a tile saw and were taking small pieces to make a mosaic across the bench, spelling out in a beautiful collage of colors: "Meleia Willis Starbuck."

The Cal football players of this next generation still walk by the bench, I'm sure, unaware of its history, toiling in a program that pays its coach $6 million, has consistently losing seasons, and graduates the lowest percent of athletes in big college football. Frat boys stumble by on late nights to and from desperate parties. The homeless sit and rest here. Immigrant students, hoping Cal will be the ticket to success for their families, hurry by. Joints are smoked. Forties are tipped. College Avenue life continues around this corner.

Every year on July 17, dozens of people are drawn back here, gathering in different combinations and at different times at "Meleia's bench." In the morning I go by the bench and do some cleaning, pull up weeds, sweep, wipe down the tiles. The old folks, parents of the kids who went through this, teachers, tend to come by early in the evening. It's not all sadness now. We are not just in silent mourning. We talk, catch up, joke . . . and inevitably we tell Meleia stories, learn how little Meleia (Mercedes' daughter, born a month after the shooting) is doing, and have a hug. Ilene and I always go and we usually see Bill Pratt, the teacher who carried that first week, as well as heroic parents who have become our lifelong friends. Flowers are there when we arrive, perhaps with a few candles. The young people tend to arrive later, at 10:00 or even midnight. They sit together, pour out devotionals, catch up, and reluctantly leave. This is how we weave our way forward, constructing a life that seeks to be worthy, at least a bit, of those lives we have lost.

Youth Poetry Teacher: Losing a Student and a Friend

Donte Clark

Donte Clark is a youth poet teacher at RAW Talent in Richmond, California.

Losing a student is something that is too real. No matter how many times the thought crossed my mind, I could never prepare for it. I am a student myself. In many ways, people are role models in my life. So I am forever a student as long as there is something to be learned and some growing for me to do. With that being said, I am also a teacher. Regardless of my age or position in life, we are both teachers and students at the same time, depending on the exchange we have with our neighbors. There is no below or above one another. We are equals. I learned that. I know that each day I leave the confines of my house I face the threat of a bullet, by a friend, a law enforcer, or aimless shootings.

As a teenager I was hanging out in places that sure enough could have gotten me killed. My many mentors and safety-keepers were horrified by the fact that they might lose me any day because of my poor choices. What I always told them was this: Just me being a Black male, I'm a dead man walking. That is how I felt. Over the years I've matured in many areas. But this thought sometimes still haunts me. No matter how positive I try to be, I live with the paranoia of being knocked down by someone who looks like me.

To go from being a high school student to becoming a spoken-word educator for high school and junior high students, I realized the impact death can have on a person's heart. To work with someone every day, encouraging them to finish school, encouraging them to leave the streets alone and find a different route. To argue with your student about making right choices and believing that they can do better is a difficult thing when you feel like you are just not reaching them. I've had many days where I felt the work I was putting in with a particular student was going to waste. Other days we laughed, joked, and opened up to one another about what scares us and what we want out of life. Having these moments and honest dialogue is what brings out the humanity in us all. I'm not viewed as an authority or a person who knows it all. I'm viewed as human, a person who makes mistakes and grows from them.

I became an older brother to this particular student, Dimarea Young. He was gunned down just before lunch hour. Dimarea and I come from the same struggle. Our stories are similar. We both at a time were caught up in the madness that plagues our community. Then we both became young people who chose to make that difference—to be someone who is productive. He was gunned down. I can't help but feel like at any time that could be me. So what do I do? Yes, outside looking in I'm considered a teacher, a positive role model. But on the inside, I feel violent. All I want to do is get even. Where I come from, getting even breeds more violence. I envision myself hurting a lot of people, sometimes not caring who it might be. Something has to be done.

I think about this young man, we grew and took something away from each other. I knew what I could have done to cope with the loss of my student, little brother. But realizing the impact my words had on this young man and other people in my community, how could I resort to violence? Dimarea and many others looked up to me, for showing the way, for encouragement to move forward, for practicing what it means to forgive yourself. As an educator it's hard to cope with such a loss, especially when you feel so connected to the root cause of violence in your community.

What I decided to do is from that moment forward is to make sure I build with those that are around me. Not to be sad and bitter about what's going on in the world, because that won't change it. I keep it in my mind to reach out to those students I see regularly and get to know them—spending that time in the workshop as a place for building, creating change in the world by nurturing those around me and prioritizing a fun environment. Making sure to honor those we've lost by putting out good work in the community that will call for action, a stop to the killings.

Losing a student is real. It pushed me to be the man that I need to be. Believe in what you teach these young people and back your word up. Young people like Dimarea believed in me because he felt connected to me. We shared the same background and had the same goals. I aided him in his times of need and I spoke against the violence. If I was to go back on my word to retaliate for his death, then all of our talks were for nothing. Whether dead or alive, he taught me what it means to practice what you preach. As an educator, I just go harder to do the work and value the time we have together.

10. What Schools Can Do

This slim volume is, by design, open-ended and tentative. There are no certainties in this dreadful art, the presiding over a community experience of death. I have resisted simple formulae partly because each situation will be different. Still, it seems like a good idea to systematize some of the main points.

- The number-one take-home is that you have to build community now to survive the crisis later. You cannot start building community when crisis strikes. All the practices you do now to enrich your classroom and school context will not only promote more engaged learning but will provide an anchor during a crisis.
- Pay attention to your students. Don't let someone fall through the cracks. Check your own prejudices that may make a student invisible. Be a lifeline before a student makes a bad choice.
- Recognize that your situation is unique. You will be improvising responses, based on the students, the community, and the kind of school culture in which you live. For this reason, your number-one skill is to listen, listen, listen; pay attention; and allow distributed leadership.
- Support teacher and student autonomy, developing habits of independent and creative thinking and planning in order to help school communities deal with crises.

- Pay attention to your own needs. Balance your own mourning and distress with your role as leader and supporter for your class. Find trusted places for respite, support, debriefing.
- Create a mutually supportive relationship between teachers and counselors. Allow counselors to have time in classrooms and get to know the students there; allow teachers to learn from the expertise of counselors.
- Create certification programs, involving continuing education credits, for general education teachers on dealing with crises, trauma, loss, and grief.
- Develop ethical norms for your school community, a community that celebrates upstanders, that stands in opposition to racism and sexism, that opposes bullying. Work for these values to be truly internalized and owned by the student and parent community, not just imposed from above.
- Allow the arts to help you and the students explore the many incomprehensible things about life and its transitions. Avoid simple certainties. Do not allow logistics to swamp the deeper contemplative work.
- Allow students space to create—memorials, poems, T-shirts, murals, whatever is needed. Allow a complete free-speech zone. Allow students space with one another, with no adults present.
- Pay attention to the problem of imposing solutions, imposing a particular ideology or religion on the students. Many will try to give comfort by giving an explanation, a certainty, about the meaning of death. Without necessarily confronting what you consider wrong moves, hold open the space of wonder and exploration for students.
- Recognize your own positionality—your own privilege or cultural assumptions or prejudices or life experiences that might hinder your ability to be completely present

and helpful for students. Practice solidarity as opposed to charity.

- Learn to understand trauma and the effects of persistent trauma. Help students to explore their circumstances in order to develop critical hope. Recognize sources or resilience and strength in your students.
- Avoid simplistic framings of tragic events, framings that suggest a simple binary, innocent angel versus evil devil. Life is always more complex than that.
- Try to understand the lives and motivations of those who transgress, who harm the community. Work and struggle with these students, too, as this is part of the educational project.

Afterword:
From the Counselor and Therapist

I have insisted that teachers are not counselors. This book is not about how to be a counselor. It is a look at the work teachers do, what we must do, in the classroom to hold the space, to help students, families, and ourselves go through this. Still, I thought it would be helpful to check in with a professional, actually a therapist from my own department, the School of Education at the University of San Francisco. We were both at a university-sponsored writing retreat at Point Reyes when I mentioned to a group that I was working on this book. Dr. Cori Bussolari, who is the coordinator of the Marriage and Family Therapy Program, spoke to me later, expressing deep interest in the project. I was delighted to get a reader who might know something, or at least might have professional knowledge of the issues into which I was digging. We ended up in some extended conversations that helped me enormously in thinking about these issues. After reading a few drafts over the next year, Dr. Bussolari wrote me the following, which I think serves as a useful Afterword to this book.

Cori Bussolari

I function within a blatant dichotomy. Most of the stories I hear in my clinical work contain elements of grief, loss, and trauma. These are the issues that cause people significant distress, bring them to therapy, and keep them coming back week after week. At the same time, however, I continue to be struck by the unfortunate observation that a concept as universal and inevitable as death is still somewhat vilified within our society. If *vilification* seems like a strong word, I don't believe it is strong enough. If we were to be truly honest, most of us would prefer not to ever hear or talk about death. We avoid and minimize and choose not to share our experiences because we don't want to make others uncomfortable; we also don't want to deal with it ourselves. Death is the equivalent of a swear word. It is a topic that we do not discuss at the dining room table, nor do we bring it up in social situations. One of my first jobs in the therapy field had me working with sick or dying children in a hospital setting. I'll never forget the moment my supervisor told me that in order to do this work, I would have to be able to conjugate and use all the forms of the verb *to die* rather than the euphemism *passed away*. This was not easy. My difficulties seemed to stem from a personal and societal belief system that death discussions are just not okay. An example of this occurred while I was riding the train a few months ago. I overheard a conversation between two women about the death of a mutual officemate due to breast cancer. They were sitting about four rows back, but were talking so loudly that I couldn't help but hear everything. Most interestingly, any time illness or death was mentioned, each one would independently lower her voice to an inaudible whisper, as if whatever they were saying were taboo. I wondered why something as inescapable as death continues to be such an unacceptable conversation.

After reading your book and having our wonderful discussion, Rick, I have become quite curious as to why we are only really just beginning to focus upon the issue of death and grief in schools. In fact, it has been only recently that am I hearing an increasing amount of discourse regarding the desire to understand and support teachers when a student death occurs, in light of the fact that teachers have always been required to manage the aftermath. It doesn't really make any sense, but in some ways it reminds me of the recent focus upon the mental health needs of groups such as

the military, police, and fire department. These people have histori-
cally dealt with the most difficult, scary, and horrific events over
and over, and yet for years, were unable to access help. In many
ways, their grief was disallowed and disenfranchised, that is, not
socially sanctioned as appropriate. The stigma of showing that one
was at all affected greatly reinforced keeping their mouths shut, as
there is a much greater societal stigma toward men who show their
emotions—a particular kind of "Don't Ask, Don't Tell." Fortunately,
this stance is changing in many ways. Their plight seems to be parallel to the gigantic expectations we have for teachers. Of course,
we assume that they are teaching the students curriculum so they
can learn and grow; that is a given. They are also expected, however,
to deal with whatever is brought into the classroom, which is quite
often related to loss, trauma, or death, especially within our urban
school districts. So the question I ask is how can one teacher hold
and support the social and emotional needs of a classroom of 30
students who are all responding to traumatic events *and* continue
to teach lesson plans *without* being taken care of themselves? Perhaps because more women than men are teachers, the expectation
of teachers as caretaking becomes a given, and an endemic part of
the job description. You ask such a simple but powerful question,
one that I feel is of ultimate importance from a mental health perspective—Who will take care of the caregivers?

I am not a teacher, Rick, and I will never know what it is like to
come to work every day charged with the responsibility of educating children. I have, however, done enough therapy with children
and adolescents and worked in enough schools to know that to
their students, teachers are much, much more than what the name
"teacher" implies. Depending upon classroom age and needs, teachers are required to wear a variety of hats with limited training. Although they are not therapists, they are often the first person a
child discloses abuse to; although not nurses, in some schools, they
take care of a sick or hurt child; although not parents, they must
provide nurturance (often feeding their students) and security; although not grief counselors, they have to take care of their students
when someone dies; as you say, they need to always "improvise."

What other profession asks their people to "wing it" over and over again? Teachers need to be all things to all students all the time. In fact, they are the primary triage manager for significant student life events without the kind of training it takes to do so—from a mental health perspective, the impact of this can be enormous.

There is a considerable amount of literature regarding *vicarious traumatization* (a term often used interchangeably with *compassion fatigue*), and I have worked with several teachers experiencing this to varying degrees over the past few years. This concept essentially asserts that people on the front lines of crisis management, such as emergency room personnel, psychotherapists, firefighters, and so on, begin to exhibit symptoms similar to those of a direct trauma, just by virtue of being exposed in a secondary manner. Although teachers might intermittently deal with large and acute traumas such as Meleia's death, they will also most definitely become the receptacle for smaller, long-term, insidious student traumas (which we in the mental health biz call "little t's"). I don't want to sound overly dramatic, but this is a big deal. We need to begin to proactively address the social and emotional realities of being a teacher. Without explicit support and good training, managing both these smaller, more frequent traumas and student death, can cause burnout, can hugely impact someone's ability to perform his or her job, and can erode physical or mental health over time. Although it's not always a clear path, a deeply committed and effective teacher can eventually feel so overwhelmed that he or she might choose to leave the profession—and I've seen it happen.

So the idea of preparedness comes to mind for me, especially regarding death. When I supervise burgeoning therapists, the first thing I suggest is this—"You need to get right with your loss experiences." What I am saying is that no matter what they do in their work, they will inescapably have to deal with death. The same holds true for teachers. Similar to a therapist's, I believe that a teacher's journey should include an exploration of their relationship to their own losses. For example, have they talked about significant areas of loss, trauma and death? What continues to be some tender areas that need further healing? What is still hard for them to address?

What would be challenging for them to hear from their students? It is clearly unfair to send people into battle without first talking about the realities of their work with complete transparency. In your book, you espouse this exact idea—let's create a conversation about what it is that teachers *really* do, so that they can envision what they need, so that society can begin to look at an ability to be strong and vulnerable at the same time as an asset, so that their grief is not diminished, so that they can ultimately create a strong holding environment for their students.

Humans grieve best when we have a community to rely upon. We become stronger. We can develop a sense of hope even in our darkest time. We are built for this, not to remain isolated and dis- connected and unsupported. When we share grief, we don't have to take everything upon ourselves, collapsing under the immense weight of it all. At the same time, it is understandable why we don't always access other people, as we don't trust that we will be sup- ported to continue our process, whatever it might be. We may not want to talk about it, but we also don't feel that others want to hear it. So often, when asked how we are doing, we respond with "I'm just fine," even though what we really want to say is "I am hurting." No matter how well you think you can avoid it, grief will "out" itself at some point. So here is the deal about death—there is no right way to grieve and no right amount of time to grieve, and everyone grieves differently. Even the most capable and stoic people feel deeply and hurt, and we need to have people around us who we trust to be there to let us do and say whatever we need without judgment. Teachers seem to have a built-in support system filled with other teachers. I hope that with this increased focus on sup- porting teachers' emotional experiences in schools, a mechanism will be developed to further access and strengthen this community to support one another—I can imagine that this could be profound.

Viktor Frankl wrote about his experiences in the Nazi concen- tration camps in one of my favorite books, *Man's Search for Mean- ing* (1984). He says, "What is to give light, must endure burning?" Here is my take: We need to acknowledge and talk about death in order to fully appreciate the life we have. The death of a child is incomprehensible and will affect the people in its orbit, but we need to get right with the idea that death is part of life and that by continuing the collusion of disenfranchisement, we can't fully thrive. Through desensitization of this difficult conversation, teachers have a better chance of focusing on student strengths and not viewing students as victims, because, you know, "they have such tough lives." Here is my wish list for teachers: required and ongoing training around student social and emotional issues, the development of a community support group structure—there are important stories to be shared, explicit conversations about the emotional realities of teaching, and lastly, psychoeducation regarding the impact of working with student death and ongoing trauma experiences. In essence, stay close to the people you trust, be kind to yourselves, and hold in your hearts the belief that grief is not a sign of weakness—you don't have to whisper.

References

Agee, J. (1957). *A death in the family*. New York, NY: Bantam Books.

Brooks, G. (1994). "Boy Breaking Glass" from *Blacks*. Chicago, IL: Third World Press.

Coates, T.-N. (2008). *The beautiful struggle*. New York, NY: Spiegel & Grau.

Duncan-Andrade, J. (2009). Note to educators: Hope required when growing roses in concrete. *Harvard Educational Review*, 79 (181–194).

Erdrich, L. (2006). *The painted drum*. New York, NY: Harper.

Frankl, V. (1984). *Man's search for meaning*. New York, NY: Washington Square Books.

Giovanni, N. (1997). *Love poems*. New York, NY: William Morrow & Co.

Glass, I. (Narrator). (2013, February 13). Harper High School, Part One. In *This American Life*. Washington, DC: National Public Radio. Available at http://www.thisamericanlife.org/radio-archives/episode/487/harper-high-school-part-one

Hansberry, L. (1959). *A raisin in the sun*. New York, NY: Vintage.

Hemon, A. (2011, June 13). The aquarium: A child's isolating illness. *The New Yorker*.

Howard, D., Feigelman, S., Li, X., Cross, S., & Rachuba, L. (2002). The relationship among violence victimization, witnessing violence, and youth distress. *Journal of Adolescent Health, 31*, 455–462.

Kurosawa, A. (Director). (1952). *Ikiru*. Tokyo, Japan: Toho Co. Ltd.

Perry, B. D., & Szalavitz, M. (2006). The boy who was raised as a dog: And other stories from a child psychiatrist's notebook. Philadelphia, PA: Basic Books.

Rodríguez, L. J. (2005). *Always running: La vida loca: Gang days in L.A.* New York, NY: Touchstone.

Rodríguez, L. J. (2001). *Hearts and hands, Creating community in violent times.* Toronto, Canada: Seven Stories Press.

Szymborska, W. (2001). The end and the beginning. *Miracle fair*, Trans. Joanna Trzeciak. New York, NY: W. W. Norton.

Ward, J. (2013). *Men we reaped*. New York, NY: Bloomsbury.

Weeks, C. (1967). *Job Corps: Dollars and dropouts*. New York, NY: Little, Brown.

Index

About the Author

Rick Ayers lives in Oakland, California with his wife Ilene. He spends time with his three children and three grandchildren as much as possible. He is an assistant professor of teacher education at the University of San Francisco in the Urban Education and Social Justice cohort. He taught in the Communication Arts and Sciences small school at Berkeley High School, where he pioneered innovative and effective strategies for academic and social success for a diverse range of students. Rick was a core team member of the Berkeley High School Diversity Project. He has his PhD from the UC Berkeley Graduate School of Education in the Language, Literacy, and Culture division. He is the co-author, with his brother William Ayers, of *Teaching the Taboo: Courage and Imagination in the Classroom* (now in it's second edition); is co-author with Amy Crawford of *Great Books for High School Kids: A Teacher's Guide to Books That Can Change Teens' Lives*; and is author of *Studs Terkel's Working: A Teaching Guide*. He works regularly with Youth Radio, Youth Speaks, Voice of Witness, and other community and arts organizations.